Be A Unicorn.

FAITH
TO INNOVATE

21st Century Tools & Strategies for Leadership Transformation

Dr. T...

Dr. Tecoy M. Porter Sr.

INNER TREASURE
PRESS

Inner Treasure
P R E S S

9532 Sabrina Lane, Elk Grove, CA. 95758
(916) 647-3064; innertreasurepress@icloud.com
ISBN: 978-1-934466-51-3

Praise for Faith To Innovate

In every role I've played, whether as a point guard in the NBA or as Mayor of California's capital city, my goal has always been to help others pursue excellence. I have witnessed Dr. Tecoy Porter, a rising star in our city; exhibit this same passion in both his words and deeds. I highly recommend his book, Faith to Innovate, as a must read for anyone desiring to do the same.

Kevin Johnson
Mayor, City of Sacramento
Three-time NBA All Star

"Change the method but keep the message" is a familiar refrain in current church circles. This book nails that with the added oomph of faith - the yeast that makes the bread rise. Faith is the key ingredient that pleases God, but how you wield it makes the difference whether it is effective or not. Dr. Porter's visionary paradigm here raises your sights to a whole new level.

Keith and Mary Hudson
Keith Hudson Ministries/Arise International
(Parents of pop star Katy Perry)

Dr. Tecoy Porter has struck a chord in his New Book - Faith To Innovate, that the Body of Christ needs to hear. Your feet will never walk where your mind has never been...therefore, it is extremely important to embrace the principles of out-of-the-box thinkers and trendsetters like Dr. Tecoy Porter. This book is a masterpiece and should be required reading for anyone in leadership.

Dr. Ben Tankard
Pastor Destiny Center Church
Grammy Winning Recording Artist / Producer
Reality TV Actor, Thicker Than Water

In over 25 years of successful business ownership, management and ministry, I have lived by the motto, "When God gives you a vision, He'll make the provision!" In his insightful book "Faith to Innovate", Dr. Tecoy Porter shares how he too has learned how to live by this same axiom and breaks down the indispensable qualities of "faith" and "innovation" so others may do the same. This is certainly a must read for any practitioner of leadership desiring to learn, grow and maximize their potential!

Dr. Teresa Hairston
Founder/Publisher emeritus of Gospel Today Magazine
President of Gospel Heritage Foundation

A successful coach is one who can assess the opposition, make key adjustments and incorporate those modifications into a winning strategy for his team. This formula for achievement is exactly what Dr. Tecoy Porter so clearly defines in his insightful new book, Faith to Innovate. Drawing from personal experiences and focused research, Dr. Porter demonstrates how an effective leader uses faith as the driving force in adapting essential new strategies. I encourage all leaders to read this book thoroughly and use it as a resource as you coach your team to success.

Dr. Dave Martin
America's #1 Christian Success Coach
Bestselling Author, Twelve Traits of the Greats

Leaders are always focused on what's next. Asking, "What is God doing now?" "How can we join?" "What is the "Aha!" we need to move us further?" In his newest book, "Faith to Innovate" Dr. Porter expertly answers these questions and more by providing innovative solutions for today's leadership challenges. Leaders need fresh vision to produce a thriving future. In his book, Dr. Porter offers the tools and strategies needed to inspire just this, making "Faith to Innovate" a must read!

Ray Johnston
Senior Pastor/Founder
Bayside Churches/ Thriving Churches International

To use an overused and yet still true adage that " the last words of a dying church are, we've never done it that way before" Sad but true in many of our churches that is the mantra as well as the mood. Over against that reality Dr. Porter dares to call the church to relevance by creative and courageous innovation. Employing not only scholarly data but biographical and transparent truth as well, Dr. Porter challenges us to more, higher and better, believing God deserves both and the times demand both. I am so glad that my friend and brother has given us this gift and challenge, I pray we receive and respond to them both.

Bishop Timothy J. Clarke
Senior Pastor
First Church of God, Columbus OH

In a time and age where "Leaders" only lead where it's convenient, safe and gainful. Bishop Porter has exemplified transformational leadership not only where it is safe, but also in the jungles of Africa, here in Uganda, we read this book while watching Dr. Porter's life on every visit. For those that really want to walk the walk - this is a must read.

Pastor Joshua Kuteesa
Senior Pastor
Mukono Prayer Palace Church International, Kampala-Uganda

The rate of change in our world continues to accelerate. Those who are unwilling or unable to adapt will be left behind. Dr. Porter's visionary book "Faith to Innovate" is a powerful tool to help leaders think through the changes that need to be made to accelerate their organization to not simply survive, but to thrive in the future.

Dr. Bryce Jessup
President Emeritus
William Jessup University

I have had the privilege to observe Dr. Tecoy Porter as a leader in our community for many years. We share a common bond having followed fathers who built a wonderful legacy of leadership and ministry. Tecoy is respected by his peers in our community and recognized as a leader. He provides a fresh perspective on leading through the current challenge of a rapidly changing culture. This book is a toolkit for leaders that will inspire and inform as we endeavor to leave a legacy of our own for those who follow. I respect Dr. Porter and value his friendship and contribution to the well-being of our community.

Rick Cole
Senior Pastor
Capital Christian Center, Sacramento, CA

To excel in the 21st century "Faith To Innovation" is a must read for those who want to be on the cutting edge in ministry. As a leader who is out on the front lines, this is my next read!

Sherwood Carthen
Founder, Former Lead Pastor
Bayside of South Sacramento (BOSS), CA
Former Chaplain for the NBA Sacramento KIngs

It's impossible to have the right answers if we keep asking the wrong questions. Dr. Porter understands this well. In a culture and church that is changing constantly, we must each learn to be futurists. The sage on the stage is dying, but the coaching leader is rising to nurture the next way of world changers. This ground-breaking book will blast you out of a stagnant past into a vibrant future.

Francis Anfuso
Co-Senior Pastor
The Rock of Roseville, Roseville, CA

We are living in a transitional period as never before. Leadership as we know it has changed and is continuously changing. I've known Dr. Porter for years and found his book to be very insightful. As a pastor of 43 years (as of May 26, 2013), I endorse this body of work to the fullest. Whoever purchases this book will have world of new insights and strategies.

Dr. Ephraim Williams
Senior Pastor
St. Paul Missionary Baptist Church Campus, Sacramento, CA

This book helps us understand that God has a Plan, Purpose and Path for the lives of this generation and for future generations to come. As a culture, let's seize the moment and embrace our destiny.

Samuel Gordon
Executive Vice President
Capital Bible College, Sacramento CA

Dr. Tecoy Porter is a positive, and encouraging Pastor who has a humble and sincere heart. It has been my pleasure to work alongside

Dr. Porter in unifying the Body of Christ in the Sacramento Region by bringing ethnic diversity and denominational streams together. A harvest of wealth may be gleaned from the tools and strategies outlined in his book, "Faith to Innovate" as the reader understands and applies biblical principles that lead to innovative leadership. If you are searching for authentic transformation in your leadership, I highly recommend this book.

Don Proctor
Lead Pastor, Impact Church, Roseville, CA
Founder, City Pastors Fellowship

This book is an excellent piece on innovative leadership. The reader will be challenged to change old ways of thinking and believing and he will be given tools to make a difference in the organization or ministry in which he serves. I have appreciated knowing and watching Dr. Tecoy Porter in his leadership of Genesis Church as well as his leadership in the Sacramento region. He has lived and continues to live out what he teaches in this timely piece that will be helpful to all who desire to better their leadership skills.

Jim Jessup
Director of Church Relations
William Jessup University

Dr. Tecoy Porter is the epitome of an upstanding leader, family man, and pastor in the community. He totally inspires me when I attend Genesis Church and listen to his sermons which are straight to the point based on the WORD of the Bible, yet funny but very real in how we need Christ to live, save our souls, and be successful. When he speaks of FAITH, he lives and breathes it daily if not hourly! I have appreciated his wisdom in his young age and sharing of his personal challenges in life that we all can relate to. This book will be nothing but a testimony of his own faith walk and how we can utilize 21st century strategic tools to becoming an innovative leader.

Pleshette Robertson,
Founder, Sacculturalhub.com
CEO/Chief Editor of THE HUB Magazine

To be able to lead in this stage of the 21st century and beyond, one has to be willing to make a shift in their process, and methodology as it pertains to how they function as a leader. Dr. Tecoy M. Porter, Sr. has given a prescription if you will, for all those who are ailing in the area of leadership. Dr. Porter, through his careful intertwining of his candid personal testimony, and the intricacies of his poignant research, gives a step-by-step manual that will open up the belief system of one who dares to transform their mind in their approach to leadership. Whether you are the executive in the boardroom, the coach on the sideline, or the pastor in the pulpit, this 21st century manual on strategic leadership will bring great innovation, as well as inspiration to revitalize and reshape those whom you lead, and bring about results of great success.

Dr. Ellington W. Porter Sr.
Senior Co-Pastor
Genesis Church, Sacramento, CA

Dr. Tecoy Porter is a leader of leaders! His knowledge and stories of the benefits of and challenges in leadership development are genuine. His ability to peel back the layers creates a level of vulnerability to which anyone can relate. He translates his experiences of leading the church and gives the reader an in-depth account that is thought-provoking and promotes self-reflection. His live presentations are no different than the words on the page; it's raw footage. If you want to innovate, read a book to which you can relate. "Faith to Innovate" IS the book.

Dr. Janice ('Jai') Armstrong
CEO, LiHK Consulting, LLC
Executive Leadership Coaching, Training, and Organizational
Development "Discover what you LiHK (like); Become who you Love"

I am greatly impressed with the leadership and style of Dr. Tecoy Porter. After watching him lead his church family back from the brink, by first trusting in the God he preaches about, remaining positive in the face of what seemed to be insurmountable odds, and leading with vision and conviction, I support and endorse this work and encourage all leaders, no matter their role, to read. Dr. Porter has through his own walk in the ministry produced a product that will both encourage and empower the reader not only to get up but to also see the possibilities and potentials that our God has for them and their ministry. I applaud Dr. Porter and thank him for his unselfish work and heart to reach out and help others in the ministry.

Rev. Darryl B. Heath, Pastor
St. John Missionary Baptist Church, Sacramento, CA
Moderator of the Northern District Baptist Association, Inc.

Table of Contents

Dedication

I dedicate this book to the memory of my parents: Dr. Robert Porter & Hazel Porter who deposited the seed of leadership in me.

I also dedicate this book to my wife, Karlette, and children, Tecoy Jr, Kamarion & Kara for the leaders you are now and will become in the future.

The Legacy Continues!

Acknowledgements

When I began this journey my children were 10, 6, and 4. Now my oldest is only a blink away from college and my two youngest are entering into their preteens. Although I've tried my hardest not to, I am sure I have missed some moments important to them during this process. Daddy thanks you for understanding and wants you to know everything I've done is for you and your future! I especially thank my wife, Karlette, who I will celebrate 21 years of "wedded bliss" by the time this is published. I am grateful for you believing in me, and especially in us, throughout all that life has thrown at us! You are my number one cheerleader! I am your number one fan! I love you! To my brother, Ellington and sister-in-love Tiwana, thanks for the unending encouragement and support towards your big brother. You all have amazed me with your faithfulness and growth throughout the years. Thanks for your willingness to stretch with me. The best is yet to come!

To Dr. Diane Wiater, PhD., thanks for your guidance and tutelage in developing and completing this manuscript and doctorate program. Thanks for being a prime example of coaching leadership. I could not have done this without you. To all of my professors and my cohort at Regent University! I miss seeing you during residency. I am proud to have learned from each one of you. Thanks for developing me into a better leader. To Dr. Janice Armstrong, so proud of you! Thanks for the push all the way through and for making me keep my end of our promise to finish together. Thanks again Deneen Brown for your expert proofing skills. Maybe now I can confidently call myself a writer.

Samuel Williams, DJ Rogers Sr., Hezekiah Walker, T.D. Jakes, Edwin Hawkins, Walter Hawkins, Aaron Lewis, Bob Harrison, Timothy Clarke, Joshua Kutessa, Sherwood Carthen, Samuel Gordon, Ephraim Williams, Yardley Griffin Sr., Don Proctor, Francis Anfuso, Rick Cole, Phillip Goudeaux Sr. and Mayor Kevin Johnson – all of you have greatly influenced me with your leadership excellence, friendship and mentorship near and afar. I am extremely grateful for each one of you and what you have contributed to my life.

Finally, to my Genesis Church family, staff and leadership, thanks for your continued trust and support. Special thanks to Lester McQuillon Sr., Joyce Taylor, Gerard Murdock, Bob Adams, Lawrence Byrd, and Yvonne Adams for your leadership, courage, and faithfulness. All of you bring out the best in me! I am humbled to serve as your Pastor.

Introduction

My Leadership Journey

"Failing forward' is the ability to get back up after you've been knocked down, learn from your mistake, and move forward in a better direction."

— John Maxwell

I guess leading came naturally to me being the eldest sibling at home and a preacher's kid. With my father being an influential pastor, I was expected to follow in his footsteps and be a leader too, in and out of the church - and for the most part I did. In middle and high school I led academically as an honor student, athletically as a captain on my football and basketball teams, and socially over my church's youth groups and choirs. As a college undergraduate I was a student leader in the African American Student Union, and the Conservatory of Music at the University of Pacific (UOP), Stockton, California. Even after I transferred to California State University of Sacramento (CSUS), I led there in many groups extracurricular and academically in my pursuit of my Bachelors of Arts in Music and Masters in Business Administration. No matter the group or organization, if I was in it, I was bound to lead it.

Once in the workplace, I led groups in the Information Technology field as a trainer, manager, and consultant in a variety of companies in Northern California. Prior to committing to ministry full time I was responsible for overseeing up to 300 Technical Support Specialists for the University of California, Davis. Call it overconfidence, youth, or just plain ignorance – most likely a mixture of all three – leadership seemed to come naturally and easily to me, that is until I became a Pastor.

Greatest Leadership Challenge

My greatest leadership challenge did not come from my secular career, but from the moment I agreed to succeed my father in the ministry and join my brother, Ellington Porter, as a part of the Senior Pastoral team of the Genesis Missionary Baptist Church. This is not to say I haven't experienced any success pastoring. Actually quite the contrary, after having come to terms with the loss of my father, and being called to the ministry, the majority of my pastoral career was a success according to almost anyone's standards.

Genesis was already a prominent church in Northern California and very well known across the nation. Due to the wisdom and leadership of my parents, Dr. Robert Porter and Hazel Porter, we inherited an organization with a solid foundation and a sizeable platform. With this head start we organized the construction of the Dr. Robert Porter Center (DRPC), a multi-million dollar, multi purpose family life center in honor of my late father in 2003. It houses our worship services, athletic leagues, and most importantly the various outreach services we provide for our community. Completion of the DRPC was such a significant milestone it not only attracted local press, but national attention with the Reverend Jesse Jackson Sr. as our featured keynote speaker for our grand opening. The new edifice also made Genesis the hot spot for musical events in the Northern CA area featuring Grammy and Stellar Award Winning Gospel Artists Hezekiah Walker, Walter Hawkins, Edwin Hawkins, Forever Jones, Beverly Crawford, the legendary DJ Rogers and many more.

As a direct result of this and other early achievements in our ministry I wrote and published a book about the lessons learned in leading our congregation to successfully undertake such a task entitled "*Releasing*

Your Inner Treasure: 8 Kingdom Keys to Unlocking the Wealth Within You." Please note we aren't your typical mega church, but a sizeable one with a mega vision! The construction of the DRPC was the result of a Living Vision originally given by my father. However, like Moses, his role was to only provide the vision for it. Thus it was up to us, his sons, to fulfill it. In order to fulfill this charge we took on the role of Joshua and Caleb to lead our spiritual family to our Promised Land. Doing so took us on a journey of self-discovery and purpose as we tapped into the hidden treasure within us to achieve such a goal. Many people doubted we could accomplish it, but through the grace of God, and the faithfulness of our congregation we were able to succeed. This was an especially humbling accomplishment which I will never forget.

From the book release and the overall success of our ministry, I was featured on top Christian media outlets Trinity Broadcast Network (TBN), Total Christian Television (TCT), Christian Television Network (CTN), LeSea Broadcasting and a host of others to speak about my book and ministry. Doors opened for me to be a contributing expert author, panelist and keynote speaker on subjects concerning leadership, finance, and personal development on national platforms. I was even recognized as an upcoming New Breed Gospel Preacher alongside such prominent honorees as TD Jakes, Billy Graham, Benny Hinn and Joel Osteen in Los Angeles, CA. From this standpoint, the choice of following my calling into pastoral ministry was a favorable one. This is not to say we didn't have our challenges. In fact, you cannot have this type of success without MAJOR challenges! We lost our fair share of battles along the way, but God remained faithful to his Word and we never lost the war!

From Rising Star to Free Fall

From 2003 – 2009, I was a rising star. The church was growing in membership, influence and wealth, and frankly, so was I. I was headed towards the next level of ministry stardom and success. Then the fall started to occur. A major shift in our local economy occurred. City and community partnerships once fruitful started to wither due to budget battles and political pressure. Jobs were becoming harder to come by.

In California, we became familiar with a once obscure term - furlough - a temporary unpaid leave for employees due to economic conditions. In our case, the company was CA's local government, the number one employer of the City of Sacramento. As a direct result of the growing unemployment, involuntary furloughs, and rate increases on subprime mortgages, the CA housing market crashed hard. Families not only were losing their income, but even more importantly their wealth! Retirement accounts were drained and equity dissipated like water in a desert due to this economic collapse.

Of course with the loss of community partnerships, growing unemployment, and skyrocketing foreclosure rates, contributions started to decline. Like other non-profits, we did our best to help our community with housing and financial workshops and other services to assist families during the downturn. However, we also had to make the hard decisions to undergo budget cuts of our own, starting with some of the outreach programs, missions, and services which were key to our earlier success. The final straw, however, was the loss of key staff. It was getting more difficult to keep some of the lead individuals who were instrumental in creating our success with diminishing resources. This led to the disillusionment of many within our membership. I wish I could say I handled this well, however, I know I didn't. Even with my best efforts I made mistakes. I lost trust.

I started falling.

A Dream Foreclosed

I'll never forget the day when I got the notice about the For Sale sign being placed in front of our church. I knew it was coming. With the decline in contributions, partnerships, and membership, it was only a matter of time as we could no longer afford the loan we secured to build our dream. We spent over a year in negotiations with the lender to no avail. Finally we found ourselves upside down on our own property. The property's value was now significantly lower than the loan amount and wasn't about to turnaround anytime soon. We had two choices! File Chapter 11 bankruptcy or allow the lender to foreclose with a temporary lease deal with hopes of repurchasing the property in the future. After much prayer and consideration, the senior leaders of the church and I chose the latter. It was one of the hardest decisions of my life! Not only had I lost both my parents, but now I stood on the verge of losing their dream and tarnishing their legacy!

I was still falling.

The Gift of Learning

One of the most cherished gifts given to me by my parents was their life long passion for learning. Both my parents never stopped learning, even when they were at the top of their respective careers. I witnessed both of my parents continue their educational pursuits long into their adulthood and careers. As a result, they were able to accomplish so much in such a short amount of time. Their example taught me a core principle of being a successful leader - leaders are life long learners. It was this lesson which brought about the inspired idea to better myself as a leader.

As I stated earlier, I realized what was working before wasn't working now. I realized it wasn't what I knew that was hindering me, but what I didn't know that kept my parishioners and me from moving forward. What was also evident to me was the fact that not everyone was losing! Somebody was winning, even in the recession! So I made the decision to go back to school to pursue a program in which the curriculum took advantage of my educational background and professional experience, yet honored my Christian values. I found exactly what I needed in the Doctor of Strategic Leadership Program at Regent University's School of Business and Leadership in Virginia Beach, Virginia.

I stopped falling.

Leadership Turnaround

The decision to go back to school to improve my leadership skills was the best decision of my life because it led to my leadership turnaround. Through my studies I not only developed my personal leadership skills, but also learned innovative leadership lessons which led to personal and organizational transformation. My choice to improve myself as a leader resulted in me becoming a better pastor, teacher, mentor, consultant, coach, husband, father, brother and friend. Because of my *Faith To Innovate*, my life and everything I'm associated with has been transformed for the better! I am no longer in free fall and my ministry is moving successfully from recession to total recovery! The following are just some of the blessings that have occurred since applying these lessons.

- The vision still lives! With tremendous support from our community and city leaders, our congregation reclaimed full ownership of our church property in September 2013! God IS Good!!
- Steady ministry growth with additional services, youth, and community outreach programs.
- We are now International with the launch of our daughter church, "The Mukono Prayer Palace Church International" in the Mukono District outside of Kampala, Uganda.
- We continue our gospel music legacy by independently releasing our latest EP "All the Way The Tribute" by The Porter Brothers & Genesis.
- Birthed new multi-cultural partnerships within the community and city, and with new evangelical organizations.
- Gained a greater sense of togetherness, purpose and vision within leadership and congregation.
- Committed to leading our city and church, innovating exciting and new concepts and ideas, into the 21st Century and beyond!

The reason why I wrote this book is so you too can achieve your leadership turnaround! You don't have to stay stuck in free fall! My goal is to assist you in your transformation to becoming the best leader you can be personally, spiritually, and professionally by providing you the tools to help you use your Faith to Innovate!

Within this book you will learn:

- Why innovation is key to being an effective leader and how to increase your capacity to innovate!
- Why it's not just about the economy and what 3 cultural trends are significantly shaping the future of the world's social, political and religious landscape.
- What a coaching leader is and why it is essential for YOU to become one.
- How you can (Re) Structure your organization's design to better lead, develop, and deploy your greatest resource – people!
- What culture is and how it is essential in the transformation process!
- Why faith is critical to all innovation and why it's suicidal to be a leader without it.

I am excited for your future and am honored to partner with you on your leadership journey! I am confident that through these lessons you too will experience the same growth and transformation as I did to become the leader you were always designed to be. Remember, authentic change always takes time. So use this as a field guide, especially during those times when you feel like you're stuck in free fall. I guarantee, if you take these lessons to heart, you will stop falling and experience the leadership turnaround you need and desire.

To Your Greater Future!
Dr. Tecoy Porter Sr.

Chapter 1

Why YOU Need to Innovate

"Innovation distinguishes between a leader and a follower."

— Steve Jobs

Since you are reading this book I assume it is because you are a leader of some kind; religiously, socially, or professionally. If so, then you are well aware of the peaks and valleys that accompany leadership. On one hand, being a leader can be an incredibly high experience because of the opportunity to bring about positive transformation in individuals and organizations. On the other hand, leadership can also be extremely challenging as best-laid plans fall apart, goals aren't achieved, and failures become more common than successes.

The challenge to lead in today's environment is even greater due to an increasingly global economy accompanied with progressive change and complexity. Now, more than ever, leaders of every organization face tremendous uncertainty in responding to a volatile environment made up of innovative technologies, emerging markets, new competition, economic turmoil and changing demographics. As such changes accelerate, so does the uncertainty. Future threats and opportunities are harder to predict, making once proven and relied on leadership approaches and strategies undependable and potentially harmful to the survival of an organization and the future of its stakeholders. Because of such complexity the quest for effective leadership is at an all time high as the demand for it becomes more and more evident.

Ironically, the world doesn't have a shortage of leaders. In fact, the desire to lead exists now more than ever due to the perceived fame, wealth and influence associated with it. In our world, leaders are winners! They are the top of the food chain! They are the most successful, powerful and influential among us all! Consequently, politicians campaign for it, pastors preach for it, businesspeople compete for it, and athletes contest for it. Hence, we have many leaders - socially, politically, and religiously, but unfortunately, little leadership. Simply put, today's leaders overall, just aren't getting the job done, making effective leadership as uncommon as it is essential.

Lack of Leadership Confidence

The lack of effective leadership is not lost on the world, especially here in the United States. According to the most recent survey by the National Leadership Index (NLI), America's confidence in their leaders has steadily decreased to its lowest levels since launching their study seven years ago. On the whole, Americans have below average confidence in their current leaders, only citing an above average rating for leaders in military and medical sectors.[1] Such findings are not surprising considering the economic meltdown of 2008, international conflicts in Iran and Afghanistan, record-breaking unemployment, escalating foreclosure rate, and congressional gridlock in Washington; it is a wonder that any optimism exists at all. However, according to the report, 78% of Americans are still optimistic that today's problems can be solved through effective leadership![2] Which brings up the question, "What can a leader do to improve their leadership and make it more effective?"

Leading Change

> *"Nothing happens without leadership.*
> *Nothing changes without leadership.*
> *Nothing develops without leadership.*

Nothing improves without leadership.
Nothing is corrected without leadership.
Everyone, everywhere, every time is always being led."
– Myles Monroe [3]

The role of the leader is to create followers. The task of the leader is to bring about constructive and necessary change. The responsibility of the leader is to bring about such change in a way that is responsive to the true and long-term needs of those who follow them. The primary reason why leaders are deemed ineffective is because of their failure of not accomplishing the task and responsibility of leading change. Primary reasons why leaders are failing in this responsibility are rooted in emotions of fear of the unknown, losing control, and, security in the status quo.

An additional reason why change is so difficult is because of the phenomenon of senior leaders not having any history of dealing with the magnitude of change happening today. Change is quicker, faster, and deeper now than any other time in recent history. Leaders who are of the Baby Boomer and early Gen X generations are used to slower-moving business and social environments with less global competition, little to no social media with stability being the norm. The ruling motto for them is "If it ain't broke, don't fix it." [4] Thus leading change for them becomes even a harder proposition than it normally is because they don't lack the experience to draw from.

Agility Gap

While the current environment calls for a more flexible approach to leadership, research indicates that most leaders never change. Data collected from over 600 leaders in a wide variety of industries revealed that 90 percent of managers operate at a lower level of leadership agility, which is best suited for relatively stable environments where complexity is low or nonexistent. As a result of their unyieldingness, a phenomenon identified as an "agility gap" is occurring between many organizations and their environments. [5]

The primary reason for the occurrence of this agility gap is the leader's inability to modify their leadership style. Hence, they continue to do what they have always done, hoping to achieve different results. They don't accept the fact that they are the cause for the inefficiencies occurring in their organization, department or group. Instead, they place the blame on the shoulders of their subordinates, accusing their lack of support, skill, or ability for the leader's ineffectiveness. Negative behaviors as these along with being autocratic, egocentric, and non-cooperative are identified as traits that contribute to ineffective leadership.[6]

While specific future developments are vague, strategic forecasters are certain of two deep trends: the pace of change will continue to increase, and the level of complexity will continue to grow.[7] Realizing this, today's leaders must shed the notion that what worked for them before will work now and instead, seek out new or modified leadership approaches and tailor them to fit the situations they face to remain effective.

Change As a Trend

Leaders who do attempt to change often make the mistake of basing their transformation off the latest trend popularized by the latest bestselling guru, be it a CEO, sports coach, celebrity or political figure. The thought is if they model them, and follow their methods then they will achieve the same results. I can't tell you how many times I've been down this road. What I have learned is while one can learn from the experiences of others, the process of doing so can be very costly and frankly a waste of time and effort as you chase the rabbit down its hole. Prepare to be disappointed if you believe the idea that one-size fits all. Leadership is too complex. The reality is what works for one will likely not work out the same way for another. Effective leadership is not just based on certain traits or skills of an individual, but is also influenced by the setting of the environment, makeup of a task, and the needs of the followers.[8] In other words, leadership just cannot be copied off of the latest fad or trend, but must be tailored for both the leader and their environment.

Change and Credibility

Change cannot happen if leadership is not deemed credible. A high level of behavioral integrity must exist in order for culture change and adaptation to effectively occur. Behavioral integrity is the perceived fit between espoused and enacted values.[9] In other words, people doing what they say they will do. The development of trust and credibility among employees or members is necessary to the maintenance of behavioral integrity, which is vital for successful change efforts in organizations. In essence, there is no way for leadership to be effective if it is not credible. Credibility is the foundation of leadership.

Desired Leadership Qualities

In the 2009 National Leadership Index (NLI) survey, six leadership qualities were identified as having the greatest impact on leadership credibility: trust, competence, working for the greater good, shared values, results, and being in touch with people's needs and concerns.[10] Leadership researchers, Kouzes and Posner also conducted a study on which qualities people looked for in leaders. After years of research, they found four top traits, which consistently scored high globally: *honesty, forward-looking, inspiring and competence.*

Honesty

Honest leaders not only tell the truth, they also live using a set of ethical principles and clear standards. Ethics refers to the code of moral principles and values that governs the behaviors of a person or group with respect to what is right or wrong. Ethical values set standards as to what is good or bad in conduct and decision-making.[11] Ethics are central to leaders because of the influence dimension. Leaders have a special responsibility because the nature of their leadership puts them in a special position in which they have a greater opportunity to influence others in significant ways.[12] Ethics is critical to effective leadership because it involves values, and one cannot be a leader without being aware of and concerned about one's own values. In other words, ethics are important to leadership because, in a way, they define how one leads.[13]

Forward-Looking

People expect leaders to have a sense of direction and a concern for the future of the organization. This expectation directly corresponds to the ability to envision a future, which connects to others' hopes and aspirations. When people share in a future vision, they are more likely to willingly follow a leader. Compared to all the other leadership qualities constituents expect, this is the one that most distinguishes leaders from other credible people.[14]

Inspiring

People expect their leaders to be enthusiastic, energetic, and positive about the future. It's not enough for a leader to have a dream. A leader must be able to communicate the vision in ways that encourage people to sign on for the duration and excite them about the cause. Leaders must uplift their constituent's spirits and give them hope if they're to voluntarily engage in challenging pursuits. Enthusiasm and excitement are essential, and they signal the leader's personal commitment to pursuing a dream. If a leader displays no passion for a cause, why should anyone else?[15]

Competent

Leadership competence refers to the leader's track record and ability to get things done. This kind of competence inspires confidence that the leaders will be able to guide the entire organization, large or small, in the direction in which it needs to go.[16]

Honesty, forward-looking, inspiring, and competence are leadership qualities that have remained constant over more than twenty-years of economic growth and recession, the surge in new technology enterprises, the birth of the World Wide Web, the further Globalization of business and industry, and the ever changing political environment.[17] In essence, these four qualities are timeless and are the foundation for credibility.

Change That Sustains

For many, innovation is equated with change. But this understanding is incomplete. Change is happening all the time whether we're aware of it or not. A random event, insight or an accident may be novel, but can't always be considered an innovation unless it's permanent. Anybody who's ever tried dieting understands this principle. Losing weight is an accomplishment, but keeping the weight off is truly life changing. The point of the principle is change is not effective unless it is sustainable. This is the reason why today's leaders must not only view themselves as change agents, but as innovators. Innovation is the key to improving one's leadership because it causes change that sustains.

A powerful way to think of innovation is *intentionally 'bringing into existence' something new that can be sustained and repeated and which has some value or utility.* That is, innovation is always related to some practical 'in-the-world' value. It is about making new tools, products or processes, bringing forth something 'new' which allows human beings to accomplish something they were not able to accomplish previously. Innovation and leadership are closely related because they both focus on bringing about a better future.[18]

Increasing Your Innovation Capacities

Being innovative is not just reserved for the Steve Jobs, Bill Gates, or Barack Obamas of the world! We all have the capacity to innovate! We all have the capability to think of new ideas, create new methods and apply new processes. Increasing this capacity is essential for leaders as you face challenges never seen before in this volatile environment. The lessons within this book will teach you how to increase your innovative leadership capacity and even more importantly, create a culture of innovation in the organizations where you serve. However, the very first step you must commit to is to commit to increasing your innovation leadership capacity. Change cannot happen in others until it happens in you! You must first make the commitment to make sustainable change as a leader. This means you must make the following commitments:

Become A Learner

The best way to stay stagnant and stuck in freefall is to stay complacent in the status quo. I know I've said it before, but I must repeat myself again. Things are not what they use to be. What worked before will not work now. Thus only leaders who commit to learning and promoting a learning culture will be effective in the 21st century and beyond. Learning and innovation ensure the renewal and survival of leaders and organizations by helping them transform themselves from within and respond responsibly to external challenges as they exploit what they have learned in the past while exploring or innovating to deal with the present and future.[19]

Embrace A Global Mindset

Globalization and its many forces are not only here, but are here to stay. Successful leaders are those who possess the ability to influence individuals, groups, organizations, and systems that have different intellectual, social, and psychological knowledge or intelligence from their own. A global mindset is the new competitive advantage in the marketplace and the difference between failing, surviving and winning![20]

Lead From The Future

Many leaders are fatalistic when it comes to the future because they believe it is what happens to them, instead of what they create. This perspective limits the ability to be proactive and seek out ways to create a chosen future.[21] To counter this, leaders must commit to developing their foresight - the ability to make decisions that are judged to be good not just in the present moment, but also in the long run. Leaders with good foresight will lead from the future by identifying and assessing a wide variety of possibilities and making astute judgments about what will work out best over time.[22]

Lead With Love

Leadership is not about perks, position or prestige, but about people. Unfortunately, too many of our leaders have forgotten about this. Consequently, more and more people are questioning the credibility of leadership because their concern for their position outweighs their concerns for those they lead. In other words, leaders do not care about the people they are leading. Successful leaders are those whose foundations are rooted in love, service and integrity. Bruce Winston calls it *Agapao* leadership – doing the right things at the right time for the right reasons.[23] Calvin Miller refers to it as servant leadership - not seeking to possess leadership, but being possessed by leadership; a calling to serve our fellow man under the direction of the spirit of Christ.[24] No matter what you decide to name it, love, service and integrity should be the primary attributes that drive your leadership!

You Can Do This!

> *Take the first step in faith.*
> *You don't have to see the whole staircase.*
> *Just take the first step.*
> *   - Martin Luther King Jr.*

The first step to becoming an innovative leader involves making a commitment to do so. To have a genuine commitment requires two things. The first is desire. The second is faith. The very fact that you have read this far is proof that you already have the desire. I know that this book has the tools and strategies to transform your leadership and I believe you already possess the skills, abilities, and passion needed to make this happen. Now it's up to you to believe and apply your faith to use all of these resources to become the leader you are destined to be! To help cement your commitment to becoming an innovative leader I have provided a Faith To Innovate Commitment agreement for you on the next page. Sign it! Once you do, you will be on your way to becoming an Innovative Leader of the 21st Century!

Faith is the key to innovation! Believing in what you are hoping for. The evidence of what is not yet seen. When you feel like giving up, use your faith to get you through! Transformational times calls for transformational leaders. I believe this is your time. Embrace it! You can do this!

Faith To Innovate Commitment

I, _____, hereby decide to become an Innovative Leader so I can bring about constructive and necessary change in a way that is responsive to the true and long-term needs of those who follow me.

I commit to the development of my innovative capacity by being a learner, embracing a global mindset, leading from the future, and leading with love! I dedicate all of my skills, abilities, passion and FAITH to transform my leadership to become an Innovative Leader of the 21st Century!

Signed this _____ day of _____ 20___ .

- -
Your Signature

Please go to www.FaithToInnovate.com to let me know of your commitment!

Think About it…

1. Increasing your innovation capacity requires bringing new thinking and different actions to how you lead. How can you think differently about your role and the challenges you and your organization face?

2. What can you do to break open entrenched, intractable problems?

3. How can you be agile and quick in the absence of information or predictability?

4. Determine at least 3 behaviors you can change or add immediately to take the first step to building up your innovative capacity. How can you measure your progress?

Chapter 2
It's Not Just The Economy...

"Innovation is the ability to see change as an opportunity - not a threat"

- Anonymous

In 1992, James Carville coined the phrase "It's the economy, stupid."[25] This simple phrase was a major driver behind why Bill Clinton became our 42nd President. Since then it seems that the relevance of this phrase has become even greater with the recent history of our economy. According to the National Bureau of Economic Research (NBER), the recession beginning December 2007 was the longest running economic downturn since the 1930s.[26] It crippled the housing market, induced unyielding unemployment, sent individuals, corporations, governments, and even cities into bankruptcy, all of which has permanently changed the way our economic system operates globally. Even I personally have suffered from the economy. My home was a part of the many which were significantly underwater and my church property fell into foreclosure. Although the economists of NBER declared the US recession officially ended in June of 2009, significant repercussions still linger across the nation and the globe to this day. No wonder they've nicknamed it The Great Recession.[27]

Of course, what we all crave is recovery. Hopefully, in the form of an economic upturn which would lead to the return of how things used to be. However, I'm afraid this dream is just that… a dream. Despite the relevance of what James Carville said in 1992 his phrase does not hold true today. Yes, we need jobs! Yes, we need to fix the housing crisis! Yes, we need an overhaul of our finance system and once these solutions occur they will bring about major relief to our economic situation. However, as much as this is true, even these solutions will not return us back to what we once called "normal". Why? Because it's not JUST the economy… *Stupid!*

A Changing Landscape

Our world is changing, and with it is America's social, political and religious landscape. The growing consensus of sociologists everywhere is this change is not just the result of recent economic swings. Instead, it is the product of a cataclysmic convergence of global cultural trends impacting the very foundations our society has been built upon. The entire landscape is changing and is never going back. Instead, we are transitioning into a new normal with a new reality being shaped by three prominent cultural trends: the Colorization of America, the Rise of the Millenials, and the Social Media Revolution.

Colorization of America

Back in the early 1990's was a popular comedy show called, "In Living Color" created by and featuring brothers Keenen and Damon Wayans. The show was groundbreaking because it was the only one of its kind featuring a predominantly African-American cast on a major television network. The title of the show, "In Living Color" referred to this distinction and its emphasis on contemporary urban subject matter. Surprisingly, the pioneering show became a mainstream hit launching the careers of Golden Globe winner Jim Carrey, Oscar winner Jamie Foxx and multiplatinum music artist Jennifer Lopez to name a few.[28] Unwittingly, the show also was a sign of the cultural demographic shift happening within America's populace.

Sociologists have created various terms like multiculturalism, cultural diversity and globalism, in attempts to describe this cultural phenomenon. Noted author Richard Rodriguez called it the "Browning of America".[29] I prefer to call it the Colorization of America in recognition and celebration of the complex cultural richness which accompanies such diversity. No matter what term you use the fact is America's future is no longer a country restricted to Black and White, but is now "Live and In Living Color!"

The Majority Minority

According to the U.S. Census Bureau, minorities now represent more than half of America's population under the age of 1, a historic demographic milestone with profound political, economic and social implications. The bureau - defining a minority as anyone who is not "single race white" and "not Hispanic" - estimates that 50.4% of children younger than 1 were minorities as of July 1, 2011, up from 49.5% from the 2010 Census taken in April 2010. Making 2011 the first time the population of infants under age 1 a majority minority.[30]

While the non-Hispanic White alone population is still numerically and proportionally the largest major race and ethnic group in the United States, it is also growing at a slower rate. During the past 10 years, it has been the Hispanic population and the Asian population that have grown considerably, in part due to relatively higher levels of immigration. Due to their diminishing rate of growth, Non-Hispanic Whites are projected to no longer make up the majority of the population by 2042 and in 2050 they will compose only 46.3% of the population. By 2042 there will be no clear ethnic majority in the country anymore.[31] In other words, we will be a majority minority nation, and will need to change the way we talk about "minorities" soon.

I'm "Cablinasian"

Before a certain world-renowned professional golfer became infamous for his extra-curricular sleeping habits, Eldrick Tont "Tiger" Woods made headlines early on for another non-golfing related action. It was his creation of the term *Cablinasian* - a syllabic abbreviation he coined from Caucasian, Black, American Indian, and Asian to describe his ethnic make up. Tiger's father Earl, a retired lieutenant colonel and Vietnam War veteran, was of African American, Native American, and possibly Chinese ancestry. His mother Kultida, originally from Thailand, is of mixed Thai, Chinese, and Dutch ancestry.[32]

The reason his choice to refer to his ethnicity in this manner was significant is because of the history of American golf as a White dominated and segregated sport. So when Tiger Woods achieves the World No. 1 ranking and becomes one of the most successful professional golfers of all time - as a person of color – Black and White America took notice. Black American's felt betrayed because it seemed as if he didn't want to use his status as the Premiere World Class Golfer on advancing race relations in America. White American's were confused as to why he didn't just admit what he apparently was – another gifted Black athlete.

Ironically, Tiger's description of his ethnicity reflects the trajectory of America's future minority majority makeup. America is no longer a nation of single races or ethnicities sharing the same space. Instead, it is both increasingly multicultural and multiracial. In the last two decades alone, the number of intermarriages in the U.S. has jumped from 300,000 to over a million. The incidence of births of mixed-race babies has multiplied 26 times as fast as that of any other group.[33] Such statistics foretell a future of a more racially diverse America, with new and growing populations playing more important roles politically and economically in years to come. The future of our nation is not just more colorful, but it is color in High Definition!

Rise of the Millennials

Born between 1980 and 2000, Millennials comprise nearly a quarter of the world population. They're the first generation to grow up surrounded by digital media. Two thirds of them used computers before the age of five. They are connected 24/7 to friends, parents, information and entertainment. Accustomed to being the center of attention, they have high expectations and clear goals. They are willing to work hard, and expect to have the support they need to achieve. They have older parents and were brought up in smaller families. One in four has at least one college-educated parent. Citizens of the world, they are the most racially and ethnically diverse generation in history.[34]

"They're sociable, optimistic, talented, well-educated, collaborative, open-minded, influential, and achievement-

oriented. They've always felt sought after, needed, and indispensable. They are arriving in the workplace with higher expectations than any generation before them — and they're so well connected that, if an employer doesn't match those expectations, they can tell thousands of their cohorts with one click of the mouse. They're the Millennial Generation... nearly as large as the Baby Boom, and they're charged with potential." [35]

Millennials wield incredible market clout simply because of their number.

Beyond their actual number, however, the clout Millennials hold is a direct result of the way their perception of the world and their role in it was shaped during their formative years. Millennials were taught by their parents and teachers to view their world differently. They were conditioned to think of themselves as unique individuals who could achieve anything they wanted by simply focusing on whatever it was they wanted to achieve. At the same time they were taught that the world was full of unique people just like them and that understanding that required them to be inclusive and tolerant of other races, religions, and sexual orientations. [36]

Clash of the Generations

For the first time in modern history, workplace demographics now span four generations: Veterans (1922-1945), Baby Boomers (1946-1964), Generation X (1965-1980), and Millennials (1980-2000). Because each of the generations came of age in a distinct and unique era, each has its own perspective on such critical issues as leadership, communication, problem solving, and decision-making. [37]

1. **Veterans** born between 1922 and 1945 (52 million people). This cohort was born before or during World War II. Earliest experiences are associated with this world event. Some also remember the Great Depression.

2. **The Baby Boomers**, born between 1946 and 1964 (77 million people). This generation was born during or after World War II

and was raised in an era of extreme optimism, opportunity and progress. Boomers, for the most part, grew up in two-parent households, with safe schools, job security and post-war prosperity. They represent just under half of all U.S. workers. On the job, they value loyalty, respect the organizational hierarchy and generally wait their turn for advancement.

3. **Generation X,** born between 1965 and 1979 (70.1 million people). These workers were born during a rapidly changing social climate and economic recession, including Asian competition. They grew up in two-career families with rising divorce rates, downsizing and the dawn of the high-tech/information age. On the job, they can be fiercely independent, like to be in control and want fast feedback.

4. **Millennials** born between 1980 and 2000 (estimated to be 80–90 million). Born to Boomer and early Gen Xer parents into our current hightech, neo-optimistic times, these are our youngest workers.[38]

Accompanying this diversity of perspectives are inevitable clashes between the generations as each struggles to figure out how each fits within this crowded and volatile environment. Generations who've grown up in the information and technological age have produced a group of independent doers and thinkers who aren't concerned with following established procedures or tradition.[39] Relationships are fluid, and loyalty is conditional, based on personal values. Couple this with the fact that most Gen Xers and Millennials come in the workforce more skilled in today's technology than their predecessors, naturally challenges traditional cultural perceptions regarding hierarchical power and authority. In essence, just because a person may hold a higher position of authority doesn't mean that they will be automatically regarded as a leader.[40]

The most significant change from this generational mesh up, however, is a shift in core cultural values. What uniformly motivated us in the past, isn't so today. Members of the older generations are more likely to have a career path over a lifetime, generally prefer a 9 to 5 workday, dress more conservatively, and are intensely loyal to their workplace, religious and political affiliations. In comparison, members of the younger generations are more likely to make a statement with their apparel, prefer variable work hours, which correspond to personal needs and social commitments, and demonstrate personal loyalty to a career, or lifestyle, rather than to any organization.[41]

Generational clashes are nothing new. Conflicts replay throughout every decade as younger generations grow impatient in their leadership aspirations while older generations desperately hold on to them. No generation is better or worse than another, and prevailing attitudes are neither right nor wrong—just decidedly different. Learning how to work, live and play together is crucial, and every leader must master ways to bridge generational gaps. Innovative leadership calls for a coordinated, collaborative strategy to leverage each generation's strengths and neutralize its liabilities.

Social Media Revolution

There is no question of the major impact that technology is having on the globe today. The impact of the Internet alone has revolutionized the way we communicate, entertain, educate, govern, and even manage our finances. This trend has been accelerated with the advent of smartphones and tablets, which take advantage of wireless networks to stream information and content instantly, no matter the location. Though the influence of technology is hardly news breaking, what is newsworthy is how pervasive the use of social media is becoming globally.[42]

Social networking sites started as early as 1997 with "sixdegrees. com"[43], and they grew on. Notable among them are Six Degrees, Live Journal, Friendster, LinkedIn, Hi5, MySpace, Orkut, Facebook, Yahoo!360, Twitter, etc. Some endured. Some did not.[44] Topping the online social networks is "Facebook" which launched in 2004. In October 2012, Facebook topped 1 billion active users. More than half of them use Facebook on a mobile device. If Facebook was a country, it would be the third largest in the world only behind China (population: 1.34 billion) and India (population: 1.17 billion). Facebook is the most popular social network in every country of the world, with the exceptions of China, Japan, Russia, South Korea and Vietnam. Twitter comes in 2nd with over half a billion registered profiles, with over 100 million in the USA alone.[45]

Organizations don't have the choice on whether or not they do social media; the choice is on how well they do it. Now, with a touch or click of a button, any customer can tell all of their 300+ friends, colleagues and family how much they love a company and product or service immediately from their phone.[46]

More Popular Than Porn

In less than three years social networking became the most popular activity on the Web, supplanting pornography for the first time in Internet history. Even search engines weren't powerful enough to do that.[47] The reason for social media's meteoric popularity is primarily due to satisfying the age-old need of humans to communicate and connect with one another. Being social is fundamental to the nature of human beings. We want to use whatever channels we have to communicate, whether it is smoke signals or the net.[48] Through social media it is as easy to communicate with a person half way around the globe as it is with our neighbors next door. No one is "out of touch" unless they really want to be. In addition to the proliferation of e-readers, smart phones, tablets, and whatever future gadget or gizmo on the horizon, it is easier to communicate quickly now more than ever before.

Personalized Information

Another reason for social media's popularity is its ability to personalize information. Before social media, people didn't have much control over what information or news they received because it was held by a few and distributed to millions. Today, we are in a world where the information is held by millions and distributed to a few in which we can filter.[49] Instead of being overloaded by junk information, we now can get more of the type of information deemed relevant to our personal interests from sources we trust - family and friends. Today's breaking news doesn't occur over the television or radio, but now comes in a Twitter feed or a Facebook post. Instead of relying on movie critics or restaurant experts for the best recommendations or reviews, people search for what their friends or followers think about such things. People care more about what their friends and peers like more than what any critic or news organization because it is personal and most likely better suits their tastes.

Leading From The Future

Understanding how the Colorization of America, Rise of the Millenials, and The Social Revolution – along with the economy and other cultural trends - are shaping our new reality is key for leaders to being effective. No longer can leaders afford to make future plans based on past performance and trends or on just the economy because simply what worked before will not work today. The landscape has changed and will continue to do so. Only by broadening our perception to see "the big picture" through these cultural trends can we anticipate the future and create the appropriate scenarios to take advantage of it. The question is, "Are you willing to broaden your perception beyond your current reality?" If so, you will then develop your foresight and start leading from the future.

Think About It...

1. List five or more ways on how the three culture trends: Colorization of America, Rise of the Millenials, and The Social Revolution are impacting your particular industry or profession?

2. What additional trends do you see impacting your industry or profession?

3. What possible scenarios can you come up with for the future of your industry or profession in the next 10 years?

4. Based off your scenarios what can you do today as a leader to start preparing for the future?

Chapter 3

The Future of Faith

"Christianity as we've known it is dead... and must be embraced."

- Gabe Lyons

In July of 2012, Chick-fil-A President Dan Cathy ignited a cultural media storm after stating in an interview that he and his company "operate on biblical principles" and "are very much supportive of the biblical definition of the family unit." Defining Chick-fil-A as "a family business," Dan Cathy went on to say that "We intend to stay the course. ... We know that it might not be popular with everyone, but thank the Lord, we live in a country where we can share our values and operate on biblical principles."[50] News of Cathy's statements quickly spread through major news media outlets as CNN, Los Angeles Times, Washington Post, Atlanta Journal-Constitution, Associated Press and Huffington Post, further criticizing his biblical stance.

These and other comments by Cathy concerning his support for traditional marriage sparked the call for a national boycott on the chicken franchise from individuals and organizations advocating gay marriage. Vehement criticism was also expressed by elected officials notably in Chicago, Boston and New York who publically pledged to deny the company access to their cities because of Cathy's views – ironically all in the name of tolerance, openness and inclusion.

In response to the criticism the company issued a statement telling its customers that "going forward, our intent is to leave the policy debate over same-sex marriage to the government and political arena" and that its tradition is "to treat every person with honor, dignity and respect -- regardless of their belief, race, creed, sexual orientation or gender." It also noted that it has applied "biblically-based principles" to business management and will continue to do so.[51]

No matter what side of the Chick-fil-A scandal you fall on. One cannot help but be a little surprised as to why there was a scandal in the first place. Finding out that Chick-fil-A's leaders take their Christian values seriously is not new information. They are known to openly share how their faith influences their business. Chick-fil-A stores are one of a few major companies who still close down their operations each Sunday, a tradition started by the company's legendary founder Truett Cathy based on his Christian beliefs. So why would it be so controversial that a Christian company would support traditional marriage?

The criticism Chick-fil-A received wasn't based on them doing anything illegal in their hiring practices. There were no complaints about abusive or discriminatory behavior towards gay employees or anything else of the sort. Instead, Chick-fil-A's troubles were based simply on a longstanding belief system that has become somewhat unpopular in our present culture. According to Gabe Lyons, author of *The Next Christians* the Chick-fil-A's controversy is simply a sign of the times and a signal of a new reality that is shaping the future environment in which Christians are just beginning to face now and will continue to do so in a greater degree in the next 20 years.[52] Social scholars believe this new reality as a coming end of American Christianity as we know it and the advent of a New Era of Faith.

Shaping this new reality are 3 cultural forces, I call the 3P's: Pluralistic, Postmodern and Post-Christian.

The 3P's Of The New Future

Pluralistic

Pluralism is defined as a condition in which numerous distinct ethnic, religious, or cultural groups are present and tolerated within a society. Pluralism rather than Christianity now marks America's public square and will continue to do so in the future. Our nation is rediscovering and redefining religious liberty. Christianity's firm grip as the arbitrator of morality in our nation has given way to an open playing field for the spiritually curious. Religions once shunned like Buddhism and Islam are now gaining ground in popularity. America has become the world's most religiously diverse nation, and while Christians - in general - still make up the majority in America, overt Christian influence is fading into the background.[53]

Post Modern

In this time of uncertainty, postmodern thinking has thrived. Stanley Grenz defines postmodernism as "a questioning, and even rejection, of the Enlightenment project and the foundational assumptions upon which it was built, namely, that knowledge is certain, objective and inherently good. Consequently it marks the end of a single worldview.[54] This postmodern age is one of relativity and subjectivity. There is no concept of error or wrong in the postmodern vocabulary with one exception, it is wrong to say that someone's worldview, religion, culture, philosophy or experience is wrong. In other words, it is an error to say that someone is in error. Such thinking has brought about a skepticism and cynicism towards Christianity. In fact a recent research poll by the Barna Group revealed Skeptics as the fastest growing faith group in America. Comprised of the combination of atheists and agnostics, the segment has doubled in size in the last 25 years.[55]

Post-Christian

With such trends as cultural plurality and postmodernist thinking, America's future is becoming more and more Post-Christian. According to David. T Olsen, author of *The American Church in Crisis*, "the church has lost its place in the center of public life both physically and conceptually. By the end of the era of modernity in the mid-twentieth century, the Christian faith was no longer the center of Western culture and the church had become regulated to the margins of life and activity." [56] Consequently, the American Christian church is increasingly losing its social, moral and even spiritual influence as the United States becomes more global in daily life.

The Pew Research Center supports these findings by reporting that the United States lost its Protestant majority in October 2012, with only 48% Americans identifying themselves as such - the first time in America's history. The primary reason for this milestone is the rising number of Americans with no religious affiliation.[57] While the category as defined by Pew researchers includes atheists, it also encompasses majorities of people who say they believe in God, and a notable minority who pray daily or consider themselves "spiritual" but not "religious." Still, Pew found overall that most of the unaffiliated aren't actively seeking another religious home, indicating that their ties with organized religion are permanently broken.[58] Barna's research also revealed various measures which indicates that Americans remain deeply interested in connecting with God, but fewer and fewer retain enthusiasm about doing so in a conventional Christian church setting or through long-standing religious institutions.[59]

Christianity Is Risky Business

The 3 P's has made Christianity risky business in the 21st century. The uncertainty of the religious landscape has already brought on some startling statistics concerning the state of American churches. In the 1990s about 3,200 churches closed each year–or 1.1 percent of U.S. Christian congregations. In the 2000s, it increased to 3,700 a year and climbing. There is also a current trend of low numeric growth in church congregations.[60] Other key statistics showing the effects of these forces are:

- Only 15% of churches in the United States are growing and just 2.2% of those are growing by conversion growth.

- The number of people in America that do not attend church has doubled in the past 15 years.

- 10,000 churches in America disappeared in a five-year period.

- 1,400 pastors in America leaving the ministry monthly.[61]

Such statistics on the state of the church and its leadership leads one to wonder, "What does the future hold for the American Church?"

The Future Of The American Church

The most pressing issue any ministry may face today is presenting the Gospel in a way that doesn't change the message, but resonates with this generation in a way they will respond to it.

– Joel Osteen

Christian leaders really have two options regarding the future of the church, which are to either embrace or adapt or to resist and run the risk of dying out entirely. In other words, innovate or die! Unfortunately, the Western church is known for being slow to change, and address cultural and social realities. A primary reason for this is because we are comfortable with the status quo and the illusion of security and control it provides. While many haven't yet responded and unfortunately are actively resisting this new normal, there are those who are willing to take the risk of adapting in hopes of developing a way to stay relevant to current and future generations.

Lyons believes this new future provides the Western Church the opportunity to emerge with a new type of Christian practice that engages the culture, and restores it back to the Kingdom of God in every area and aspect socially, economically, politically and spiritually.[62] Biblical sociologist, Sam Rainer III predicts, "while the 'traditional' homogenous church will continue to decline, the churches who seek to become more culturally diverse, focused on teaching deep theological truths with an emphasis on effective ministries to families will explode."

In order for churches to thrive in the future they must commit to embracing a new today by creating an adaptive culture. Creating an adaptive culture does not mean compromising biblical truth. But involves having a thorough understanding of how cultural trends influence the message and mission of Christianity in order to adjust our methodology to best suit the environment. However, while the methods may change, the message must always stay the same.

No matter what the future holds, I believe it is the certainty of God's unlimited love for mankind that will eventually attract people who tire of the uncertainty that accompanies a pluralistic, postmodern, and post-Christian environment. The question that we all must answer is will we be ready to embrace them when they come?

Exercise #1
Making Your Church (Organization) Future Ready

While we aren't able to accurately predict the future of the church, the good news is that we can make a very informed guess by identifying how emerging trends and forces will influence our churches 10 to 20 years from now. The following exercise is one you want to do with your leadership to develop ideas on how you all can make your church future ready.

1. Break off into groups. Have each group identify and describe emerging trends, constants (things that are not changing) and issues within a particular category. Come up with 1-2 major trends/issues. Categories are:
    a. Social
    b. Technological
    c. Economics
    d. Environmental
    e. Political

2. Select 1 to 2 major trends/issues from the categories above. Think through possible impacts of current trends or potential future events upon the church in the next 10-15 years.

3. Discuss how the trends' implications influence the future strategy of the church.

4. Create ideas on how the church can adjust its strategy to better accommodate the future.

5. What can you as a leader do to better prepare yourself for the future?

6. How can you help your leadership team prepare?

Chapter 4

Introducing The Coaching Leader

"Coaching will become the model for leaders in the future."
– Warren Bennis

In our generation, a paradigm shift is occurring in the way leadership is developed and applied. The way one leads and the way they learn how to lead is already quite different than it was a few decades ago. Due to the tsunami of globalism and accelerated technology, top-down organizational systems are giving way to team models that empower more people to lead, in a much wider variety of roles. Much more than in the past, effective leadership means influencing and empowering instead of telling them what to do or simply doing the work yourself. In short, effective leadership today means being a coach.[63]

Coaching was once the exclusive perk of key executives and rising stars, but it is now becoming a standard component in the organizational toolkit to help employees, managers, supervisors, and executives in their personal development and their contribution to an organization's success.[64] Jack Welch, former CEO of General Electric states, "In the future, people who are not coaches will not be promoted." Leadership Scholar Warren Bennis posits, "Coaching will become the model for leaders in the future." A primary factor driving the popularity of coaching is how it facilitates change on a personal level, on an organizational level, and on a relationship level. In recent years, employee engagement and culture change have emerged as core initiatives for organizations as the need to learn how to maximize performance levels at minimal costs became more necessary.[65] To this end, coaching has emerged in playing a critical role by providing leaders a methodology that empowers and enables people to develop and express their intellectual, emotional, and creative capital. The key to leading effectively today is by coaching people to tap into and unleash their highest and best potentials. The aim of this chapter is to show why becoming a Coaching Leader is essential to leading in the 21st century and practicing the highest level of innovative leadership.

What Is Coaching?

The International Coaching Federation defines coaching as partnering with clients in a thought-provoking and creative process that inspires them to maximize their personal and professional potential. Coaches help others set goals, brainstorm options, overcome obstacles, take action, and utilize support and accountability. They do this not by giving advice but by listening, asking great questions, and by playing the role of a thought partner.[66]

Coaching is often compared with the practices of counseling, mentoring and consulting. However, there are a few differences between counseling, mentoring, consulting and coaching that distinguishes one from the other.

Counseling

The purpose of counseling is for the counselor to diagnosis the client's emotional or psychological state to help the client become whole. Counseling tends to concentrate on helping people get well by fixing past issues affecting current behavior.

Mentoring

In a mentoring relationship, the focus of the work is primarily on succession preparation and training. An experienced executive serving as a mentor helps a more junior staff member learn the ropes by sharing their learning and experience. The mentor has the answers and provides guidance and wisdom to help their colleague advance successfully in an organization.

Consulting

Consultants are retained for the purpose of accessing specialized expertise in a specific profession or technology. The consultant is hired to provide real time solutions for specialized problems. While consulting approaches vary widely, it is the assumption and expectation of them to provide answers and advice.

Coaching

The essence of coaching is the art and practice of guiding a person or group from where they are toward the greater competence and fulfillment that they desire. Coaches are change experts who help people take responsibility and act to maximize their own potential.[67] This is not to suggest that coaching is "superior" to any of these other methodologies. In fact, mentoring, counseling and consulting are very useful approaches that leaders will use at times. Which approach you use is dependent upon the people and/or situation you are working with and the goals you are attempting to accomplish.

What Is A Coaching Leader?

A Coaching Leader is an executive, supervisor, manager, pastor, team lead, etc., who uses coaching to invest in their people so that they grow in every area of their lives.[68] In other words, a coaching leader helps others win! This is accomplished through:
- Engaging workers, volunteers and members;
- Listening without judgment;
- Asking questions for improvement & development;
- Seeking ways to empowers others;
- Holding people accountable to their commitments and for their actions.

The reason why the practice of leadership is often abused is because most people who hold these positions don't understand their primary role. When one is asked what they believe the role of leadership is, the typical responses often include the following - someone who:

- Provides direction/vision for others
- Sets goals and makes plans
- Oversees the work
- Allocates resources
- Solves problems

While all of these answers are true, they don't accurately represent a leader's primary role. A more accurate explanation is one posed by management guru Ferdinand Fournies, *"Management is the intervention of getting things done through others."* [69] Another noted management expert and former President of the American Management Association, Lawrence Appley stated it this way, *"When you do things yourself you are a technician, when you get things done through others you are a manager."*

Unfortunately most people who are in leadership roles suffer from *"technicianitis"*. They believe their success is based on how well they employ their skills, talents, and expertise rather than those of their workers. They don't understand that a leader's effectiveness is not measured by how well they perform - individually - but how well they get others to perform. The mark of a true leader is not how well YOU get things done, but how well you get things done through OTHERS! Your role is to do everything in your power to help them be as successful as they can be. Because you succeed only when they succeed! [70] This is what coaching leaders are all about!

Why Become A Coaching Leader

As you begin to understand what a coaching leader is, you may still wonder why you should become one - especially if your current leadership style is working. You may ask, "Why fix what isn't broken?" Well the fact of the matter is that times are changing and trends don't lie. As noted before, our world is changing right before our eyes by three primary cultural forces, globalism, technology and the advent of a younger generation entering into the workforce *(see Chapter 3)*. The impacts of these cultural changes – along with major shifts in the economy - are not only deep but also far reaching. Accompanying these changes are new ideals and expectations regarding the way we work, live and relate with others on a global scale, all of which places a greater demand on how individuals lead today and in the future.

Coaching leadership is ideal because it's a model that readily adapts to this new reality by firstly exhibiting and applying the desired traits of effective leaders: i.e. honesty, forward looking, inspiring and competence *(see Chapter 2);* transcending differences by focusing on personal and professional development; and by adding value to workers at all levels. In recent years, coaching has also proven itself to be not just something that is "nice to do", but an organizational imperative for leaders by significantly optimizing both individual and team performance.

Impact Of Coaching Organizationally

Coaching has been linked to higher productivity, building a stronger culture, heightened creativity, and increased levels of employee engagement and commitment in organizations.[71] According to the 2009 *ICF Global Coaching Client Study,* companies that use or have used professional coaching for business reasons have seen a median return on investment of seven times their initial investment. Individual clients reported a median return on investment of 3.44 times their investment.[72]

Coaching also helps with a variety of goal areas. Findings from the 2010 *ICF Global Consumer Awareness Study,* showed that more than two-fifths (42.6 percent) of respondents who had experienced coaching chose "optimize individual and/or team performance" as their motivation for being coached. This reason ranked highest followed by "expand professional career opportunities" at 38.8 percent and "improve business management strategies" at 36.1 percent. Other more personal motivations like "increase self-esteem/self-confidence" and "manage work/life balance" rated fourth and fifth to round out the top five motivation areas.[73] Such findings as this and more are making the case qualitatively and quantitatively for how coaching is a worthwhile investment for individuals and organizations.

What Makes Coaching Leadership Work

Builds Relationships

In virtually every dimension of Western life outside of business, there has been a remarkable shift from autocratic – command and control style - relationships to much more collaborative ones. This is true of marriages, parenting, education, and even our local political processes.[74] A fundamental competency of coaching is co-creating the relationship. It requires that the coach shows their ability to create a safe, supportive environment that produces ongoing mutual respect and trust along with the ability to be fully conscious and create spontaneous relationship with the client, employing a style that is open, flexible and confident.[75] Building relationships is essential to leadership now more than ever because it is the key to establishing trust and credibility.

As a leader your ability to compel others to follow you simply because you are the leader isn't what it used to be. People expect to be listened to. They want to have a say, to understand the vision and have the chance to buy into it – much more than they did a generation ago or two generations ago. Positional authority works in times of crisis, but when used as a matter of course it erodes your ability to lead over the long haul. In this generation, if you cannot lead by influence, you cannot lead.[76] Such is done only through the establishment of mutual trust and credibility. Since coaching is all about building relationships it is uniquely suited to our times and generation.

Facilitates Authentic Change

In the traditional advice-giving model it is believed that the best way to help you change is by giving you wise counsel about what to do with your life, job, task, or relationship – in a convincing way, so that you'll make the decision to change.[77] However, any supervisor, manager, or parent - especially of teenagers – understands this to not be true. People don't change because they are told to change. Instead, people change when they feel the need to do so. When others request or demand for us to make changes that we do not genuinely want to make, any behavior change is likely to be either temporary or carried out as a result of a sense of compliance, not commitment. The reason for this is because it is simply not our decision. There is no ownership, thus no genuine motivation.

In contrast, the coaching model believes that the best way to help you change is to create a structured, supportive relationship that helps you take responsibility for your actions and make the changes you want to make. This approach is based off the principle that people can and should solve their own problems.[78]

Making major changes in our behaviors is not easy; in fact, change typically requires a great deal of effort. However, when people are committed to the change they want to make, it is absolutely possible. The key to realizing long lasting significant change individually is not by people being told how to change, but people becoming aware of the need to change and then deciding to act on this need – on their own, then and only then will real change happen.

Develops Leaders

The very definition of coaching is about growing and developing other people. In order to do so, people need to think for themselves and make increasingly complex decisions in ever-changing environments. Through coaching, leaders help their direct reports, peers, partners, and bosses to solve problems on their own, with higher levels of sophistication, accuracy, and productivity.[79] Developing this skillset is important organizationally because it increases a leader's leverage by empowering people to take action independently and thus multiplying leadership at various levels.[80]

Giving responsibility to others instead of taking responsibility for them is key to developing leaders because a person's leadership capacity is directly tied to their capacity for responsibility. In order to grow as a leader, a person must gradually increase in their ability to take initiative and bear responsibility. The more responsibility a person can manage, the greater the sphere of influence one is ready for. Keeping clients responsible is an intentional strategy for fostering leadership growth.[81]

Creates A Culture Of Champions

The ultimate benefit of coaching leadership is that it is a recipe for creating a culture of champions. Think about it. What if your company, church, team or group could be one built on a foundation of mutual trust and respect, with people who are able to think for themselves, more innovative in their approach to problem solving, resilient in the face of change, and seek the initiative to solve and address problems even when challenged with ambiguity or incomplete information? How would you feel being able to lead such a group of people? How would your approach to work be? How do you think the people you lead will feel about their work and your leadership? The answer is in one word - CHAMPIONS!

This is not just a pie-in-the–sky illustration of what could be, but instead of what is occurring right now in all types of organizations across the globe. There are people just like you and organizations just like yours who have learned how to thrive in this environment through coaching. Coaching is their key to winning and could be yours too! Coaching creates champions!

Pay Now or Pay Later

Becoming a coaching leader and creating a coaching culture is not without its challenges. Many managers feel they cannot afford to take the time needed to develop the trust, rapport, and personal relationships essential to coaching.

Coaching is essentially a slower approach in contrast to the fast-paced, bottom line, results now mentality fundamental to our western corporate culture.

Another challenge for integrating coaching into an organization's culture is that most managers have not been trained in effective coaching practices and very few leaders have coaches to help coach them on how to become better ones.[82] As a result, there is a misunderstanding of what it truly takes to become an effective coaching leader and to create a coaching culture.

While these challenges are daunting, they pale in comparison to the result of doing nothing to change your current situation. Think of it this way. Most of the times leaders find themselves spending their day constantly putting out fires and mopping up leaks. In fact, they are so busy doing this that they don't have time to discover the source of the fires or leaks they're putting out. Eventually, leaders will miss putting out a fire and/or mopping up a leak and find themselves in an irrecoverable situation – a firestorm or a flood. Such is the classic "pay now or pay later" situation. Coaching is a way of fixing problems at their source before they become irrecoverable. There is always a cost to doing something new. However, the cost to learn how to become a coaching leader and implement a coaching culture is most likely going to be much cheaper (and more worthwhile) then what it will cost you in not doing so in the long run.

The reality of today's world is that the rules have drastically changed. The processes that people previously used to achieve their objectives are increasingly becoming no longer valid and the traditional roles and working relationships are no longer effective. Coaching leadership is not only key to surviving this new world, but to thriving in it.

Think About It…

To be a coaching leader requires not only a change in skillset, but in mindset. The following questions are to help determine what your current state of mind is regarding your leadership role.

1. Briefly describe how you currently see your leadership role. For example: solution provider, coordinator, manager, etc.

2. Now describe how your leadership approach would change when practiced from a coaching leadership context.

3. The hardest part of being a coaching leader is not giving advice of the solution. It requires time, patience and restraint. Next time you have a chance to meet with a co-worker try the following:
   a. Ask Questions. Try to get to the source of the issue your discussing.
   b. Really Listen. Resist the urge to not provide an answer or solution. You have to believe they know the answer to the issue, they just need your permission to act on it.
   c. Set a goal or course of action.
   d. Hold them accountable:

4. Support with follow up. Schedule a time to check their progress. Support them in their journey. Remember the purpose of the is really about challenging your leadership approach and changing your mindset.

Chapter 5
Coaching Leader's Toolkit

"Knowledge speaks, but wisdom listens."

– Jimi Hendrix

Ok, I am a little embarrassed to admit this, but I used to be a huge Donald Trump fan! Really! As an MBA alum, he was the prime example of what it meant to be a successful business leader in Western society – successful billionaire real estate tycoon with a huge name brand, a Park Avenue address, not to mention the hit TV show, AND a clothing line… what was there not to like? So when I began my career, as a leader I was of the notion that I had to be like "TRUMP" - always in control, decisive, even sometimes demanding, and have all of the answers – or at least access to them. It was my way or the highway. Do what I say or "You're Fired!!"

Frankly, my Trump-like leadership approach worked most of the time during both my secular career as a high level manager and even early on as a Senior Pastor. This is not to say I didn't respect people or intentionally abused my authority. I just did what I was taught in business school. The best way to lead and get things done was by being in charge, which usually meant a lot of lecturing, directing, and telling everyone what and how to do their jobs, and how blessed they were to have me as their awesome leader. Admittedly, I was very good at it. I was highly educated with an equally high ego and motivated with an "I know what's best" mentality.

While it's upsetting to think I actually acted and thought this way, what is even more concerning is I am not the only one who believed in this top down, autocratic style of leadership. In fact, this "Trump" style of leadership is so much the standard for most leaders that it is considered traditional. Your ideal leader may not be "the Donald" or anyone like him; in fact it may be someone quite the opposite as Mahatma Gandhi or Dr. Martin Luther King Jr. However, even with this so, I bet you are still guilty of "doing the Donald" as a leader because of how much it is ingrained in our culture.

The problem with the traditional top down style of leadership TODAY is that it is quickly becoming more and more ineffective. It's old school leadership in a new school world! The best leaders in workplaces have learned how to empower and motivate their people rather than trying to control them. One reason— today's younger workforce (comprised of Gen Y/Millenials) is quite different than past generations (vets and baby boomers). They have different expectations of their leaders and workplaces. Generally, to motivate today's younger worker requires more personal attention, recognition and tolerance on the part of management *(see Chapter - Its Not Just the Economy...)*. This is where coaching leadership steps in. A recent study conducted in a large, progressive global pharmaceutical company where the set of competencies for leadership were compared with the competencies of a coach. The result? Seventy-five per cent of the competencies were the same. To be an effective leader you must be an effective coach. [83]

While there is always someone successful with the top down approach more and more leaders are recognizing this need to adjust to be more effective. However, doing so requires more than just picking up new leadership tips, tricks and skills. What it requires is a leadership makeover in your abilities, attitude and behavior. Becoming an innovative leader requires a change in both skillset and mindset. You must let go of once successful lessons, traits, and techniques that are no longer effective to implement new ones. You have to be willing to say *"Out with the old, in with the new."*

Change the Way You Communicate

As you can see by now, leading as a coach means letting go of the traditional notion of command and control leadership and accepting the idea of leadership being a shared responsibility and opportunity. As stated earlier, such a notion requires a change in mindset and the mastery of a new set of skills focused on developing those you lead. The foremost of these is in the way we communicate.

Great leaders are great listeners! Extraordinary men and women solicit feedback, listen to opinions, and act on that intelligence. Listening skills have always been important, but are even more so when leading today's generation. Recently researchers at Hudson, a staffing and executive search firm, conducted a survey of 2,000 employees across multiple generations. Beyond formal reviews, one-quarter (24 percent) of both Generations X and Y workers said they would like feedback from their boss at least once a week, if not every day. Comparatively, only one-fifth of Baby Boomers want feedback that frequently, and just 11 percent of Traditionalists would like that level of communication.[84] Clearly, times have changed and so have employee attitudes. Today's workers want to be asked for feedback and they want to be heard.

Unfortunately, being a really good listener is challenging for most leaders because it's not what we've been rewarded for. Most of us have reached our places of leadership as a result of the advice we give, the direction we provide, and the decisions we make. So many of us, whether we own our businesses or lead a department, ministry, or group have relied heavily on our ability to communicate in an instructional way, a very one-sided process. We'll observe a situation; think through all of the aspects of the problem, crisis, or opportunity, then inform our workers/volunteers on what they should do.[85]

Leaders who take on the coaching role sign up to deliberately help others succeed, but their usual way of doing this may not be a good fit for those they're helping. If leaders limit themselves to telling others how they did it, they're staying in the teacher or mentor role instead of moving into the coach role. While it is essential for every leader to possess an instructional skill set, the innovative coaching leader should equally possess the ability to engage others in order to draw from their experiences, skills, knowledge and ideas. Improving their listening skills and questioning skills accomplishes this.

Realize You Aren't A Good Listener

Everybody knows how to listen. Thus most people believe they are good at it. However, nothing could be further from the truth. The reality is most people are terrible listeners – including you. The foremost reason is because we listen for the wrong purpose. Most people view the time they spend listening as just "the waiting period" spent until it is their turn to speak again.[86] For example, have you ever been in the situation when you are talking to someone and you KNOW you are not being heard? If you are married or in a long-term relationship, then I am sure you have shared this experience. You are in a conversation, trying to communicate something very important to you and the listener. Only to find out after you have said your peace, they did not hear one word that you said. You know this because their response totally did not relate to what you said. Like you, I have not only experienced it, but I am guilty of doing this!

Researchers define this type of listening as Level 1 listening. At Level 1, our awareness is on ourselves. We listen to the words of the other person, but our attention is on what it means to us personally. At Level I, the spotlight is on "me": my thoughts, my judgments, my feelings, and my conclusions about myself and others, not on the listener.[87] In essence, if the focus of your listening is all about you, then you are listening at Level 1 and are a bad listener.

Active Listening

In contrast of Level 1 listening is Active Listening. Any message a person tries to get across usually has two components: the content of the message and the feeling or attitude underlying this content. Both are important; both give the message meaning. It is this total meaning of the message that leaders try to understand through active listening.[88]

Coaching scholars called this type of listening as Level 2 Focused Listening. At Level II, the focus is sharply on the other person. Sometimes you can see it in each person's posture: both leaning forward, looking intently at each other. There is a great deal of attention on the other person and not much awareness of the outside world.[89] Authors Kimsey-House and Sandahl describe Level 2 listening like this:

> When you listen at Level II, your awareness is totally on your clients. You listen for their words, their expressions, their emotions, everything they bring. You notice what they say, how they say it. You notice what they don't say. You see their smiles or hear the tears in their voices. You listen for what they value. You listen for their vision, for the unique way they look at the world. You listen for what makes them come and what makes them go dead or withdraw. Energy and information come from the client. These are processed by the coach and reflected back. At Level II, the impact of awareness is on the client. The coach is like a perfect mirror that absorbs none of the light; what comes from the client is returned. At Level II, coaches are constantly aware of the impact their listening is having on their clients—not constantly monitoring the impact, but aware.[90]

Such occasions are so rare that most people first find it a little uncomfortable being listened to in this manner. However, it is only at this level where authentic engagement happens and people really feel that they are heard.

Ask Powerful Questions

An essential component of Active listening is asking questions. However, they are not just any questions, but powerful ones. What you may be wondering is "what makes a question powerful?" Well questions are actually powerful in and of themselves. Questions can jump start creativity, challenge perspective, confront belief systems, and call people to action. Asking questions moves us beyond passive acceptance of what others say, or staying stuck in present circumstances, to aggressively applying our creative ability to a particular problem.[91]

Questions become more powerful through a coaching leader because of their intent on helping others reach their potential. Powerful questioning enables the leader to go from head to heart by peeling back the layers, to get to the core of performance issues, and to reveal limiting beliefs.[92]

In my experience as a coaching leader, I have learned what we often believe is the issue or problem needing to be dealt with is actually not the problem at all. Rather, it is a symptom of a deeper matter that would most likely be overlooked if approached through advice telling and traditional problem solving. Such techniques only place a band-aid on a wound instead of treating it so that it may heal.

Habits change only when convictions change or are clarified. Most people will not change their habits simply because they have the right advice. They won't make a change until they have hurt enough, heard enough, or had enough—all heart-level experiences. Powerful questioning enables you to probe a little deeper to help others identify roadblocks, what's holding them back, or to suggest specific strategies or actions that will enable them to become more professionally and personally successful.[93] In other words, the right question at the right time will bring about the right change in someone's life. This is the power of questions!

The Coaching Conversation

Active listening and powerful questions are the building blocks of a coaching conversation. Coaching conversations differ from typical, spur-of-the-moment conversations by being highly intentional and focused on the other person with the sole purpose of stimulating growth and change. Active listening and asking powerful questions are the primary tools used to move the conversation forward without telling and allowing the client to discover the answers and make choices for themselves.[94]

The endpoint of a coaching conversation is always an action step. Once a goal has been set and strategies discussed, the coach's job is to help the client translate that goal into concrete action steps. Once the client has committed to a course of action, the coaching leader is responsible for providing the on-going support needed to give the coachee the best possible chance to succeed. Providing this support is what makes this coaching skillset so valuable because it is through this action of accountability that brings about sustainable change.[95]

The GROW Model

There are many tools available to use as models for developing and implementing effective coaching conversation. One tool I highly recommend is the GROW Model. The model was originally developed in the 1980s by performance coach Sir John Whitmore[96], although other coaches, such as Alan Fine and Graham Alexander, have also helped to develop it. GROW is an acronym standing for Goal – Current Reality – Options – Will. The model is a simple yet powerful framework for structuring a coaching or mentoring session.

A good way of thinking about the GROW Model is to think about how you'd plan a journey. First, you decide where you are going (the goal), and establish where you currently are (your current reality). You then explore various routes (the options) to your destination. In the final step, establishing the will, you ensure that you're committed to making the journey, and are prepared for the obstacles that you could meet on the way.

Heart – The Key to Effective Coaching

While learning and developing the skills of active listening and asking powerful questions in a coaching conversation framework is essential to becoming an effective coaching leader, they alone will not give you the one critical attribute of coaching. As you have probably noticed by now, coaching leadership is a slower process than the fast-paced, fire-fighting mentality you are used to. Coaching leadership requires you to slow down, listen more deeply, learn, and become less reactive. It requires more patience than you are accustomed to in developing your relationships and interpersonal communications. It also requires a significant mindset shift from being "The Boss" to being "The Coach" as your working relationships become more egalitarian and less autocratic. To do this successfully requires great humility and sacrifice on your part. In other words, the key to effective coaching is heart.

Eddie Robinson, former Head Football Coach of Grambling University and one of only four football coaches to win over 300 games is quoted saying, *"Coaching is a profession of love. You can't coach people unless you love them."*[97] While this may sound odd in your particular field or profession, Coach Robinson's wisdom still holds true. You cannot be an effective coach unless you value the people you lead. [98]

Psychologist Carl Rogers refers to this attribute as holding others with *unconditional positive regard* - the basic acceptance and support of a person regardless of what the person says or does.[99] This is an attitude of grace, an attitude that values others even after knowing their failings. It is also the belief that all people have the internal resources required for personal growth.

Rogers' *unconditional positive regard* reminds me of God's *unconditional love* towards us. While it may be far reaching to expect us mere mortals to act in such a God like fashion in our work environments, we cannot escape the truth within this principle. Authentic transformation happens through love. If you seek to truly become a coaching leader and cause significant change, you must lead with your heart! Lead with love!

Coaching Leadership Development Tips

Here are three things you can begin doing today to be a better coach. Try them and monitor the reactions to see if there is a difference in others as a result of a difference in you.

1. Listen

In your next one-on-one conversations, try really listening with your whole concentration on what is being said. What is the story being told? What is the underlying message? Mirror back what is being said to be sure you understand. Remove distractions. Don't jump in to solve the problem. Make eye contact and notice body language.

2. Silence

We are usually in such a hurry that we see silence as a waste of valuable time. As a result, we often move too quickly to a conclusion. We are impatient for a solution. Rather than filling the silence, let it be. Try leaving pauses before responding. Use this silent time to really think about what you want to say rather than formulating your answers and questions while the person is still speaking.

3. Unconditional Positive Regard
We have often made up our minds about a person or an issue before the conversation starts. Try letting go of assumptions and just holding the person in positive regard. This doesn't mean you have to agree with everything they say, but it does mean that you value them as a human being and value their opinions even though they differ from yours.

These coaching techniques are more challenging than they sound. If you master them, you will find the results are well worth the effort. So I encourage you to give it a try, to act, to experiment, to just do it.

Exercise #2
GROW Model Guide
Use the following steps to structure a coaching session:

1. *Establish the Goal:*

First, with your team member, you must define and agree the goal or outcome to be achieved. You should help your team member define a goal that is specific, measurable and realistic.

In doing this, it is useful to ask questions like:
"How will you know that you have achieved that goal?"
"How will you know the problem is solved?"

2. *Examine Current Reality:*

Next, ask your team member to describe their Current Reality. This is a very important step: Too often, people try to solve a problem without fully considering their starting point, and often they are missing some of the information they need to solve the problem effectively.

As the team member tells you about his or her Current Reality, the solution may start to emerge.

Useful coaching questions include:
"What is happening now?"
"What, who, when, how often?"
"What is the effect or result of that?"

3. *Explore the Options:*

Once you and your team member have explored the Current Reality, it's time to explore what is possible – meaning, all the many possible options you have for solving the problem. Help your team member generate as many good options as possible, and discuss these.

By all means, offer your own suggestions. But let your team member offer his or hers first, and let him or her do most of the talking.

Typical questions used to establish the options are:
> *"What else could you do?"*
> *"What if this or that constraint were removed?*
> *"What are the benefits and downsides of each option?"*
> *"What factors will you use to weigh the options?"*

4. Establish the Will:

By examining Current Reality and exploring the Options, your team member will now have a good idea of how he or she can achieve their Goal. That's great – but in itself, this may not be enough! So your final step as coach is to get your team member to commit to specific action. In so doing, you will help the team member establish his or her will and motivation.

Useful questions:
> *"So what will you do now, and when?*
> *"What could stop you from moving forward?"*
> *"And how will you overcome it?"*
> *"Will this address your goal?"*
> *"How likely is this option to succeed?"*
> *"What else will you do?"*

Go to www.FaithToInnovate.com for more tools and information on Coaching Leadership.

Chapter 6
(Re) Structuring For A Change

"You can't substitute talent for structure. You need to add structure to talent to go to the next level."

– T.D. Jakes

A Pastor friend asked me to meet with him and his team about restructuring their church's music department. They were starting from scratch and wanted advice on how to revamp their music program to attract the right people, motivate its leaders and members, and facilitate the growth of the church overall. Immediately, I asked about the Pastor's vision for the church overall and what his strategy was to make it happen. He and his team shared their plans, which involved streamlining their worship services, and implementing new programs to develop their lay leadership. Then I started asking questions about the structure of the revamped ministry. The following is a portion of our conversation:

Me: So how many groups/choirs do you have in the music ministry?

Pastor/Team: Male Chorus, Woman's Choir, Youth Choir, Children's Choir, & Mass Choir.

Me: Are each their own separate entity?

Pastor/Team: Yes, except for the Mass choir. It's a combination of all choirs.

Me: Great, so describe your leadership structure. How many leadership positions do you have for each choir?

Pastor/Team: Well, there is the Choir Director, Musician, President, Vice-president, Secretary, and Sergeant-at-arms… for EACH group.

Me: How many members do you think you will have when you start the ministry?

Pastor/Team: 15… 20 at the most for each choir.

Me: How many attend your services?

Pastor/Team: Approximately 60 on average.

Me: Well… you have a whole lot of leaders (and choirs) for the size of the ministry and church. Have you considered simplifying the structure by combining the choirs and reducing the amount of leadership positions?

Pastor/Team: No, haven't thought about that. We were just planning to do what we've been doing. But how will we keep people accountable? Won't we lose control?

Me: Well… what do you want the most… change or control?

An Overlooked Change Tool

A critical mistake leaders make in their plans on creating change is overlooking the influence their organization's structure has on its goals. An organization is only as successful as its design. It doesn't matter how talented, knowledgeable, or committed its workers and/or volunteers are, if a company's organizational structure does not facilitate their growth and development then it will ultimately fail. The lack of alignment between structure and strategy is the primary reason why many organizations are having trouble surviving – and much less thriving – in today's volatile environment.

This is what became evident to me when consulting the Pastor and his team. The new ministry's structure was not aligned with the Pastor's vision and strategy for growth. While he desired to revamp the ministry as a key growth area for the church, its' structure didn't reflect it. Instead, it was an out-of-date design intended more so for control rather than growth. It was top heavy, with a disproportioned amount of groups and leadership positions to members. Every leadership function had a position which created a "too many Chiefs and no Indians" scenario, leaving the potential for conflict in the future. I pointed this out and advised them to consider simplifying the structure of the revamped ministry to align it with his vision for growth.

The Role of Organizational Structure

The responsibility of leadership is to position their organizations for success by establishing goals and strategies that keep them competitive. To achieve these goals, individual work needs to be coordinated and managed, while strategies are developed to enable the organization to readily adapt to its changing environment. An organization's structure is vital in achieving this coordination, as it specifies reporting relationships (who reports to whom), delineates formal communication channels, and describes how separate actions of individuals are linked together. An organization's structure is also essential for how organizations relate to elements outside of its boundaries such as industry, government, customers, supplier and its competition.[100]

Organizational structure is the anatomy of a company, providing a foundation within which the organization functions. Organizational structure affects the behavior of its members in the same manner as a physical structure. Buildings have halls, stairways, entries, exits, walls, and roofs, all of which influence the activities of the people within it. While not as apparent as that of a building, scholars believe that an organization's structure is equally pervasive.[101]

Value of Organizational Structure

The primary value of structure is that it channels the right resources to the right place at the right time to generate the right results. This process is often referred to as "alignment." The resources of manpower, money, management, and ministry must be aligned with the vision of leadership to achieve the goals of the organization.[102]

Due to today's volatile environment where instability is the norm, the last remaining source of truly sustainable competitive advantage lies in the unique ways in which each organization's structure is designed.[103] Today's global environment makes organizational design more than simply rearranging boxes and lines on an organizational chart. Instead, it has become an invaluable tool for reshaping the overall look and feel of an organization and a critical skill for top leaders to develop to design their organizations in ways that unleash and exploit their competitive strengths.[104]

Biblical Support For Organizational Design

Scripture supports and demonstrates the value of organizational structure and design. In the Old Testament, Moses organized Israel into units of thousands, hundreds, fifties, and tens to better manage the fledgling nation (Exodus 18:20-27). Nehemiah is shown using organizational principles to deploy people, resources and processes to rebuild the walls and gates of Jerusalem after returning from exile (Nehemiah 2-3). In the New Testament, the Book of Acts reveals the early church structure and how it began to evolve as the Christian church movement grew. Paul continued to add to the church's early structure by establishing principles regarding elders, deacons and other leaders in the Gentile churches in his letters to Timothy and Titus. Scripture does not decree that any one organizational structure is better than another, but it is clear that order, responsibility, and decision making need to be present, and that the members of the body should function according to their gifts.[105]

Although there is scriptural precedence for organizational structure in the church, there are those who don't like to discuss the need for organizational design, or in most cases, redesign, believing that doing so somehow discredit's the church's spiritual role or moral position.[106] However, by not doing so fails to recognize the growing complexity of ministering in the 21st century.

Structural Fundamentals

Tall and Centralized

Organizations can function within a number of different structures, each possessing distinct advantages and disadvantages. Traditionally, the most common organizational structure has been the tall and centralized in which activities are grouped together by common work from the bottom to the top of the organization. Made popular in during the Industrial age of the late 20th Century, this structure is more of what we think of when we visualize an organizational chart with the CEO at the top and multiple levels of management.[107] Generally little collaboration occurs across functional departments, and the whole organization is coordinated and controlled through the hierarchy, with decision-making authority residing with upper-level managers. In this structure communication tends to follow formal channels and employees are given specific job descriptions delineating their roles and responsibilities.[108]

The pros of this model lie in its clarity and managerial control. The narrow span of control allows for close supervision of employees. Tall structures provide a clear, distinct layers with obvious lines of responsibility and control and a clear promotion structure. Challenges begin when a structure gets too large and tall. Communication begins to take too long to travel through all the levels. These communication problems impede decision-making and hinder progress. Such barriers inhibit entrepreneurial action and discourage the use of individual initiative on the part of workers.[109]

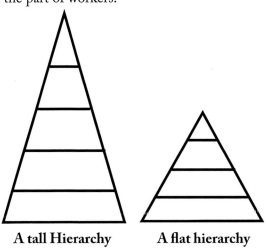

A tall Hierarchy   **A flat hierarchy**

Flat and Decentralized

Early 21st century found the environment shifting significantly as the world became more global through trade and technology. Old success factors as size, role clarity, specialization and control give way to speed, flexibility, integration, and innovation. Companies responded by restructuring their organizations to a more decentralized, flat and wide approach. [110]

Decentralization eliminates the unnecessary levels of management and places authority in the hands of first-line managers and staff, increasing the span of control with more workers reporting to one manager. Decentralization also changes the flow of communication so that top management hears staff concerns and complaints in a more direct manner and management has a more hands-on approach. The hands-on approach involves less bureaucracy, which means there is a faster response to situations that demand immediate attention.[111]

Flat organizations offer more opportunities for employees to excel while promoting the larger business vision. That is, there are more people at the "top" of each level. For flat structures to work, however, leaders must share research and information instead of hoarding it. If they can manage to be open, tolerant and even vulnerable, leaders will excel in this environment. Flatter structures are flexible and better able to adapt to changes.[112]

One Size Doesn't Fit All

While the trend for today's organizations is towards organizations adopting flatter, wider, and more decentralized organizational structures, doing so is not necessarily the best solution for all. Although the intent is to create more autonomy, responsibility, and control over resources at lower levels and promote innovation and creativity, this structure runs the risks of becoming less efficient as each unit focuses more so on its own goals, rather than the goals of the company as a whole. [113]

Gareth Morgan, author of *Images Of Organization* warns that local groups must be accountable to the center in some fashion in order to prevent decentralization to becoming a chaotic process. Therefore, some large decentralized companies sometimes need to build in more centralized communication and control systems to facilitate efficiency.[114]

Hitting the right balance between decentralization and centralization is a challenge for many organizations. Therefore, it is key that decision-makers should be aware of the strengths and weaknesses of each structure in order to come up with a customizable solution.[115]

People – The Competitive Advantage

In 1959 Peter Drucker (1909-2005) coined the term "knowledge worker" to describe a new class of employee whose basic means of production was no longer capital, land, or labor but, rather, the productive use of knowledge. These talented people – also known as "professionals" - are the innovators of new business ideas. They make it possible for companies to deal with today's rapidly changing and uncertain business environment, and they produce and manage the intangible assets that are the primary way companies in a wide array of industries create value.[116]

While it is common knowledge of the tremendous benefits these self-directed individuals bring to an organization, leaders still struggle in enhancing their productivity. Most knowledge workers increasingly find their work obstructed. Creating and exchanging knowledge and intangibles through interaction with their professional peers is the very heart of what they do. Yet most of them squander endless hours searching for the knowledge they need—even within their own companies—and coordinating their work with others. [117]

To raise the productivity of professionals, organizations large and small must change their organizational structures dramatically, retaining the best of the traditional hierarchy while acknowledging the heightened value of the people who hatch ideas, innovate, and collaborate with peers to generate revenues and create value through intangible assets such as brands and networks.[118] Steps leaders can take to start this process include clearing out unproductive complexity, moving from controlling to learning and aligning strategy with structure.

Clear Unproductive Complexity

Trying to run a 21st-century company with organizational models designed for the 20th, limits its ability to perform and creates massive, unnecessary, and unproductive complexity, which frustrates workers and wastes money. The structural ailments that plague the modern corporation include hard-to-manage businesses, thick silo walls, confusing matrix structures, e-mail overload, and "undoable" jobs.[119]

If the common enemy in today's corporations is unproductive complexity, the answer then is to design companies so both hierarchy and collaboration can do their work efficiently and effectively. This requires reworking the practical nuts and bolts of organizational design to free up the wealth-creating power of a company's talented, self-directed employees.[120] Rather than using boundaries to separate people, tasks, processes, and places, organizations now need to focus on how to get through those boundaries – to move ideas, information, decisions, talent, rewards, and actions where they are most needed.[121]

Move From Controlling To Learning

In response to the need for greater fluidity and permeability leaders are restructuring their companies to be less controlling and more conducive to learning. Learning organizations promote communication and collaboration where everyone is engaged in identifying and solving problems. Thus enabling the organization to continuously experiment, innovate, and increase its capabilities.[122] Since learning is conducive to changing, then learning must be considered a life long strategy that goes beyond formal schooling. Thus organizations need to consciously become places where change is an opportunity and where people can expect to develop while they work.[123]

Align Strategy With Structure

Ultimately, the most important decision that leaders must make about structural design is finding the balance between vertical control and horizontal coordination to find the best fit between internal reporting relationships and satisfying the needs of its external environment.[124]

Leaders must make sure an organization's structure supports the mission and strategy of the organization effectively. The difference between companies who are good and great lies in how well their systems and structure undergird their strategic goals. An organizational chart is only so many lines and boxes on a piece of paper. The purpose of the structure is to encourage and direct workers into activities and communications that enable the organization to achieve its goals. While an organizational chart provides the structure, employees provide the behavior".[125]

A Worthy Process

Truly effective design is a never-ending process. Constant change in the competitive environment requires continuous modifications of strategic objectives, consequently, design too will have to keep changing to ensure that he organization remains aligned with its strategy." [126]

Organizational structure serves as a critical tool that can provide your organization a competitive advantage in today's global market. It is also a mechanism that can either promote change or make it more difficult to prosper. Therefore, it is always important for leaders to remember that no matter the design of an organization's structure, it is up to the collaboration between an organization's leadership and its people to make it happen.

Exercise #3
Steps To (Re)Structuring For A Change

1. Reassess Organizational Goals

It's hard to determine what to do if you don't know where you are going. Take the time to review current organizational goals (i.e. mission, vision, strategy…). Questions you may ask during this process include:

- What are our organization's goals?
- How effective are we in meeting our goals?
- What new goals can we create to improve our effectiveness?

2. Clear The Complexity

Over time, we tend to layer "things" on top of each other, such as adding steps to an existing process or increasing the number of layers in the organizational structure. Clear the complexity by reviewing current structure and processes to find where conditions can be streamlined. Questions you may ask during this process include:

- Is our current structure effectively supporting the leader's vision and the organization's strategic goals?
- Are there any programs, practices and/or positions that should be revamped or removed to support goals?
- Are there any facets of the organization that can be outsourced via another company or web-based product?

3. Uncover Hidden Talents And Resources

Organizations often are full of people who either are in the wrong jobs (i.e., a misfit between job and talent) or who have talents that are underutilized in their current jobs. Employers have a great opportunity now to hone in on their employees' talents and leverage them in ways that serve everyone well. Encourage people to be creative and innovative, and support their efforts. The same logic is true of other resources: most organizations can discover "hidden" resources, or those that are underutilized. The following are steps to initiate unearthing hidden treasure from your workers and volunteers:

- Find out the strengths of your workers/volunteers via interview and/or by conducting strength test and following up with a seminar.
- Review position descriptions and responsibilities. Are they accurate? How well do they match the strengths of the individual? Do you have a plan in place that promotes worker's creativity and innovation? If not, how can you incorporate one?

Go to www.FaithToInnovate.com for more tools and information on creating structural alignment within your organization.

Chapter 7

Creating Cultural Change

"A strategy that is at odds with a company's culture is doomed. Culture trumps strategy every time." [127]
- Katzenbach, Steffen, and Kronley

If you have read this far in this book, then you are serious about developing yourself to become a more innovative and effective leader. You are now more aware of your ever-changing environment and the cultural trends influencing it. You are excited about how you can help develop others by becoming a coaching leader. You have new ideas for innovative strategies for your organization to make it more conducive to your new leadership paradigm. You are a Champion of Change and are ready to take your organization to the next level! However, before you launch out with your newfound revelation, you need to learn about the one thing that can thwart your motivation, inspiration and yes, even innovation – CULTURE!

Culture – The Invisible Barrier

Culture is the set of values, norms, guiding beliefs, and understandings that is shared by members of an organization and taught to new members as the correct way to think, feel and behave. It represents the unwritten, feeling part of an organization.[128] It signifies "how things are done around here." It reflects the prevailing ideology that people carry around in their heads and conveys a sense of identity to employees or members.[129] Culture provides people with a sense of organizational identity and generates in them a commitment to beliefs and values that are larger than themselves. While everyone participates in culture, it generally goes unnoticed. It is only when leaders go against the basic cultural norms and values that they come face to face with the tangible power of this invisible barrier. [130]

Cultural Levels

Of course there are many levels of culture that influence both individual and organizational behavior. At the broadest level, a global culture such as the Far East or the West is the highest level. At a less general level are subgroups based on gender, ethnicity, race, occupation, and industry. Still less broad is the culture of a single organization.[131] Organizational culture is not only a dimension in the life of large multi-national corporations, but also in small businesses, groups, clubs, churches, nonprofit and parachurch organizations. The minute a person walks into a meeting room, store, office or sanctuary, they pick up a nonverbal message that is more powerful than such slogans as "The customer is number one"; "We exist to give extraordinary service"; "This is a friendly, family church." [132] Regardless of level or location, culture is strongly influential in determining behavior, expressing values and enabling or preventing change.

Leadership Role In Organizational Culture

Though ideas that become a part of the culture can come from anywhere within the organization, an organization's culture generally begins with a founder or early leader.[133] In the church, culture often originates with the founding pastor, who projects his or her own vision of what is right and valued and how people are to be treated. In a business it is often the founding president. In a college it is the founding principal.

One element of the mysterious quality of leadership called charisma is how it enables a leader to embed his or her fundamental assumptions or values into the organization or group.[134] This is done by whom the leader pays attention to, how the leader reacts to critical situations, whether the leader intentionally coaches other leaders, what criteria the leader uses for praising and rewarding others and on what basis the leader recruits or rejects other leaders. [135]

Though leaders create cultures by starting groups and organizations, they are governed by the group's culture once they are formed. Culture and leadership are two sides of the same coin in that leaders first create cultures when they create groups and organizations. Once cultures exist, they determine the criteria for leadership and thus determine who will or will not be a leader."[136]

Taken a step further, the culture determines if the positional leader is really the leader and what specific role he or she will play in all dimensions of the group's life. It is the unique function of leadership to perceive the functional and dysfunctional elements of the existing culture and to manage cultural evolution and change in such a way that the group can survive in a changing environment.[137] The bottom line for leaders is that if they do not become conscious of the cultures in which they are embedded, those cultures will manage them. Cultural understanding is desirable for all of us, but it is essential to leaders if they are to lead.[138]

Cultural Reaction To Change

Because of the pervasive, yet elusive nature of culture, it is not something that can be easily manipulated. Attempts to grab it and twist it into a new shape hardly work because of its intangibility. Most change efforts fail organizationally because they are treated as a technique or program, but not as a fundamental shift in the organization's direction, values, and culture.[139] Just as individuals who face threat, uncertainty, and ambiguity tend to reassert their own habituated behaviors with redoubled force, institutions also tend to respond to challenges by reasserting their core cultural values with added zeal.[140] Such is the cultural reaction to change.

My Cultural Encounter

I experienced this cultural lesson first hand after the passing of my mother, Hazel Porter in 2005. Up until then much of the changes my brother and I made, as the new Senior Pastoral team of the Genesis Church, seemed to go rather smoothly with little to no challenges. Everyone seemed to be on board with our strategic vision and was ready and willing to do whatever it took to accomplish it. Little did I realize things were going so smoothly because of the presence and influence of my mother.

As co-founder of our church she represented a tangible reminder of the founding beliefs and values instilled by her and my father in our church. She represented the church's cultural status quo. Once she passed, the level of uncertainty immediately increased. Long standing members became apprehensive over the idea of change happening without their anchor. Consequently, I found myself becoming frustrated over what were once simple tasks and leadership decisions as they became increasingly complex. I remember having to spend many hours meeting with key congregants to explain decisions and clarify vision to keep them confident in the direction of our church. All of a sudden leadership became arduous and time consuming.

During this period I became upset with certain leaders due to their constant questioning and second-guessing and started to question my own ability as a leader. In response, I did all I could to distance myself from them. I figured that if they were not for me, then they were against me. So I did my best to ignore them, to stay out of their crosshairs and not face their scrutiny. What I did not know then is the reason for what was happening was not due to my sudden lack of leadership ability, but instead my failure to recognize the cultural reaction occurring due to the unexpected loss of my mother. The cultural balance of old and new had been upset and the old guard was wondering if there was truly a place for them in the new vision.

Although I did not immediately understand all of what was occurring with our church's culture at the time, I did know my current decision to ignore them was wrong and did not reflect my intentions. The last thing I wanted to do was to disrespect the people who labored along side my parents to establish our ministry. Plus I knew I needed their influence to move forward. So I decided to stop ignoring them and instead do all I could to involve them in the change process.

Change Process Model

There are many models scholars have developed to describe the change process. Most are based upon the change theory model developed by German-American psychologist Kurt Lewin (1890-1947). In it he theorized change as a three-stage process. The first stage is "unfreezing". It involves overcoming inertia and dismantling the existing "mind set". The second stage is when the actual change occurs. This is typically a period of confusion and transition. The third and final stage is "freezing" also known as "refreezing". During this stage the new mindset is crystallizing and one's comfort level is returning to previous levels.[141]

While Lewin's model is useful in framing a process of change which is easy for people to understand, I have expanded on it to better describe the steps needed to implement cultural change organizationally: *1. Assess Cultural Strengths & Weaknesses; 2. Create A Sense Of Urgency; 3. Recruit A Team; 4. Develop a Compelling Vision and Strategy; 5. Make the Change; 6. Make It Stick.*

Steps to implementing Cultural Change

1. Assess Cultural Strengths & Weaknesses

A common mistake leaders make in implementing change efforts is totally focusing on the weaknesses of the current culture to justify the need for change. It is important to realize, however, that every company culture has assets. Every corporate culture is a product of good intentions that evolved in unexpected ways and will have many strengths. If you can find ways to demonstrate the relevance of the original values and share stories that illustrate why people believe in them, they can still serve your company well. Acknowledging the existing culture's assets will also make major change feel less like a top-down imposition and more like a shared evolution. The key to creating cultural change effectively is by making the most of its positive elements to work with and within the culture, rather than fighting against it.[142]

2. Create A Sense Of Urgency

As Change Champion, complacency is your biggest enemy. The unfortunate reality is that most organizations don't see the need to change until it is too late. They believe that since it was good enough then, it is good enough for now and the future. The best technique to fighting complacency is by creating a strong sense of urgency for change.

Creating a strong sense of urgency usually demands bold or even risky actions that may be associated with what is considered poor leadership. Essentially, reducing complacency means initially creating conflict and anxiety to make people uncomfortable in the status quo, and hopefully motivated enough to adopt new ideas to change it.[143] This is not to advise that you commit sabotage. Instead, it is letting go of the pressure of being superhuman by allowing some things to break and not flying in to save the day. For example, you allow a financial loss to show up on the records at the next board meeting, or allow an error to blow up instead of correcting it at the last minute. The unfortunate truth is that it usually takes a crisis to inspire people to change. The best crisis is always putting a spotlight on reality.

3. Recruit A Team

Although you are responsible for initiating change, you don't want to make the mistake to implement it alone. Successful change is both top down and bottom up. It is top down because senior leadership provides vision and structure for change. However, it must be bottom up too because it is through the ranks that you get buy in and support.[144]

For some, the notion of pursuing certain persons of influence to be on your team is unattractive. You would rather ignore them than invite them into a place of power. Believe me I've been there. They might not say much of anything at all in a meeting, but they will definitely get their opinion out after, in the parking lot, or on the phone. The best way to stop this is to invite them into the change process early on. Getting their buy in and support is crucial to lowering initial resistance. So ignoring them is not an option! Many times, they really want to just be involved and just don't know how to show it. If this isn't the case, your public invite nullifies their private criticisms.

4. Develop A Compelling Vision And Strategy

All successful transformations have one thing in common, a compelling vision and strategy. In the initial step, you highlighted the crisis to get them on board. Now, you must develop and emphasize the solution; a vision of how the future can be better and strategies on how to get there.[145] This involves finding the right ideas and aligning them with the goals of the church and the needs of those involved.

The reason why this step is crucial is because authentic change requires sacrifice from all involved. Change often demands things getting worse before they get better while having to do more with less. Such demands result in the loss of certainty and security that will threaten to defeat the transformational process if there is no hopeful vision to pursue. Formulating and articulating a compelling vision and strategy that will guide the change process is vital to overcoming burnout, uncertainty and fear along the way. Successfully doing this is the difference between an average leader and a transformational one.

5. Make The Change

This is the transitional stage of the change process. When new ideas are implemented such as adding new products or services, changing worship styles, or implementing a new organizational structure. The key in this stage is to show your commitment to the change. It is critical that you model the change in every way through both communication and actions.[146]

Even more important than what is said is what is done. Leaders who transform their organizations "walk the talk." They seek to become a living example of the new corporate culture that the vision aspires to. Nothing undermines a communication program more quickly than inconsistent actions by leadership. Nothing speaks as powerfully as someone who is backing up their words with behavior. When an entire team of senior management starts behaving differently and embodies the change they want to see, it sends a powerful message to the entire organization. These actions increase motivation, inspire confidence and decrease cynicism.[147]

6.   Make It Stick

In my leadership as Senior Pastor, I've led many change efforts both large and small from contemporizing our worship style, adding services and ministries, to constructing new facilities. Although varied, one common lesson that I've learned from each experience is that no change will stick without follow through. Ironically, the goal of the change you are implementing is to ultimately replace an old tradition with a new one. This is what Lewin refers to as the refreeze stage of the change process.[148] Where the change becomes institutionalized into the culture of the organization to the point where it becomes the new tradition.

Realities of Cultural Change

Slower Than You Think

Change occurs in chunks, too fast at one moment, while agonizingly slow in another. Although creating an atmosphere of high expectation is necessary initially, it's vital to understand that it doesn't reflect the reality of the change process. Significant change is mostly incremental and methodical, and will always encounter more resistance than expected. The key is to not succumb to the pressure of high expectations and to always remember that change is a process that requires management to be sustained.[149]

People Join In Waves

Some will respond readily to change and are stimulated by it, while others view change in a threatening way. Roger's 'Innovation Adoption Curve' shows five typical reactions to innovations. Within a common umbrella strategy, each group needs to be treated in somewhat different ways. It is particularly valuable to target and get on board with the early adopters and those more ready to change:

- Innovators (2.5% of the population) – people leading the change

- Early adopters (13.5%) – people willing to try out new ideas but in a cautious way

- Early majority (34%) – people who accept change more quickly than the average

- Late majority (34%) – skeptics who resist change as long as possible

- Laggards (16%) – people who are set in 'the old ways' and hold out against change as long as possible.[150]

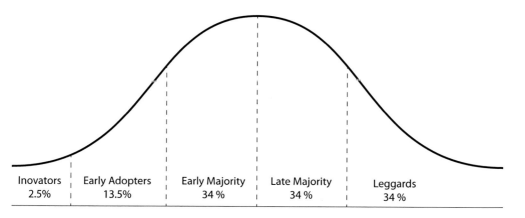

Inovators	Early Adopters	Early Majority	Late Majority	Leggards
2.5%	13.5%	34 %	34 %	34 %

Often Requires New People

Sometimes direct change in a culture can be promoted by introducing new people in leadership, by promoting maverick individuals from within and, more especially, people from outside who hold slightly different assumptions. The appointment of a new pastor, a new assistant, a new board chairperson, or a new president is an opportunity for cultural change.[151]

Cultural Change Comes Last

Culture changes only after a leader has successfully altered people's actions, after the new behavior produces some group benefit for a period of time, and after people see the connection between the new actions and the performance improvement. Without personal behavioral change on the part of organizational members, organizational culture change will not happen.[152]

Ignoring Culture – Not An Option

Ignoring culture is like driving down the highway and taking your hands off the steering wheel. You may have started out in the right direction, but eventually the vehicle will quickly veer off in unintended directions.[153] Understanding the role culture plays in an organization and how it can be used to implement effective change is critical for today's leaders. Like Christ, who came into our culture, understood, and related to us, we too must strive to lead in the same way. It is essential to our success. The leader who understands and adapts to the organizational culture is more likely to lead their organization forward and enjoy the journey.

Exercise #4
Create Your Cultural Blueprint For Change

1. Assess Cultural Strengths & Weaknesses

What are the strengths and weaknesses of your current culture? List them out to determine what practices, policies, and programs you would like to continue in the future and what new things you would like to implement.

2. Create A Sense Of Urgency

What is your reason for desiring change in your organization? Determine the ways you can raise the urgency level in your organization to create awareness and desire for change. Consider both the external and internal forces happening that are impacting your organization's environment (i.e. industry, city, country, economy, culturally).

3. Recruit A Team

List the key influencers of your organization? Develop a plan on how you can recruit them as early adopters of your change initiative. What do you need to do to get their initial buy-in? Review your list to make sure you have "credible" people and not just "yes" people.

4. Develop a Compelling Vision and Strategy

What is your vision for change? How is it anchored in your current culture? What specific items or areas would you like to see changed? What are your goals? Are they S.M.A.R.T. (specific, measurable, attainable, relevant, timely)? How do the old and new guard fit into your vision and strategy?

5. Make the Change

What new behaviors do you need to practice to sustain the change your making? What is your plan for future resistance?

6. Make It Stick

Do you have the right systems and structures in place to support the changes made? What new projects, strategies and people do you need to fortify the change?

Chapter 8
Faith, Balloons & Unicorns

"Faith doesn't make things easy, it makes them possible."
– Author Unknown

Have you heard the story about The Balloon Factory and the Unicorn? It goes like this:

"I'm not sure you've ever visited a balloon factory. Probably not. The people who work in the factory are timid. Afraid, even. They're very concerned about pins, needles, and porcupines. They don't like sudden changes in temperature. Sharp objects are a problem as well.

The balloon factory isn't really a bad place to work if you rationalize a bit. It's steady work, with a bit of a rush around New Year's. The rest of the time it's quiet and peaceful and not so scary.

Except when the unicorn shows up.

At first the balloon factory folks shush the unicorn and warn him away. That often works. But sometimes, the unicorn ignores them and wanders into the factory anyway. That's when everyone runs for cover.

It's amazingly easy for a unicorn to completely disrupt a balloon factory. That's because the factory is organized around a single idea, the idea of soft, quiet stability. The unicorn changes all that." [154]

The story of The Balloon Factory and the Unicorn is a modern day parable of what it means to challenge the status quo. The balloon factory represents the status quo – steady, quiet, and predictable. Supporters of the status quo do not want any change disturbing "the way things are done here" and will do anything they can to protect their current existence. All is well in the balloon factory until the Unicorn comes. The Unicorn represents change. It is the ultimate disruptor to the status quo and is not really liked in balloon factories. Well guess what – leader? You are the Unicorn!

The Essence of Leadership

The essence of leadership is about moving a group of people from one state of existence to a better, greater and more advanced state of existence.[155] Unfortunately, most people in leadership misunderstand their role. They believe their job is to maintain the status quo instead of changing it. Though this may have been okay in the past, this is certainly not true today or in the future. Leaders lead! You are not leading if nothing is changing! This is what this book is all about – to equip you to better fulfill your role as an innovative leader, a game changer, and ultimate disruptor. The question you must answer now is, "Are you ready to pop some balloons?" If you answered, "Yes", then you must embrace the one quality that will enable you to do this successfully – FAITH!

An Underrated Quality

Faith is often an underrated quality of leadership. This is so because faith is often masked by other notable attributes like tenacity, drive, spirit, charisma, determination, motivation, or ambition. However, none of these qualities can exist without faith.

Faith is the strong unshakeable belief in something or someone, especially without proof or evidence.[156] Faith is an inner attitude, conviction or trust. In religious traditions it is the inner certainty or attitude of love granted by God himself. In Christian theology, faith is the divinely inspired human response to God's historical revelation through Jesus Christ.[157] I personally favor how the writers of Hebrews define faith as, *"the substance of things hoped for, the evidence of things not seen (Hebrews 11:1, NKJV)."*

This scripture says to me, *"faith is the passport to a better state of being."* You can learn all of the latest techniques and implement the most innovative of programs, but if you attempt to implement any of it without faith then you will ultimately fail. Where there is no faith, there is no potential for hope. Hope for a better future, a superior process, a bigger dream, or a greater purpose. You simply cannot lead without faith, because without it, there is no place to go.

The Certainty of Adversity

A common mistake you cannot afford to make is to underestimate the amount of resistance you will encounter during the change process. Although you are now equipped with proven strategies, processes, and skills, everyone will not share your passion of innovative leadership. There is no amount of numbers, figures, charts and presentations, which can persuade all of the balloon factory workers to join you on your innovation journey. Those who oppose you will use tactics like busyness, company policy, doubt, fear, packed schedules, and a host of others – to block you from disrupting their balloon factory. While such efforts seem juvenile, they should not be overlooked. These challenges are real and have stopped many leaders dead in their tracks. Some have even led to the unfortunate decline of their organizations.

Resistance and adversity will not go away for leaders. In fact, they will most likely increase due to the ease leaders can be exposed through today's technology. Now every decision and action you make is immediately open to scrutiny and criticism by anyone AND their 300 closest friends.[158] I state this not to frighten you, but to make you aware so you can prepare. The best way to prepare for this certainty is by building up your faith.

Building Up Your Faith

While resistance and adversity are inevitable for leaders, it is also certain that both can be overcome by faith. In Romans 12:31, Paul reveals to his readers how *"God has given each of us a measure of faith."* In other words, you and I already have enough faith to accomplish everything God has purposed in our hearts and minds to do. We already possess the right amount of faith needed to successfully deal with whatever obstacles we face. Our job then, is to build up our faith. Facing adversity and resistance head on is essential in building up our faith.

Like our muscles use resistance to get stronger, so does our faith. The more resistance it encounters, the stronger it gets. The converse of this also holds true – less resistance leads to weak faith. Understanding that resistance build faith allows you to put adversity in its rightful place. Adversity is not meant to destroy you, but to build you. You will not know how strong your faith is until it is challenged in a big way. It is only through these challenges or tests that you will develop you faith and discover newfound strength.

Know Your WHY

An essential element needed for you to successfully build your faith is knowing your WHY. Knowing your WHY will provide you clarity of purpose. What is your WHY? Why does your organization need to change? Why do YOU want to cause this change? You do not want to undertake any change effort just to be doing it. Your efforts cannot be the results of just following the latest fad or trend. You must have a clear purpose. You have to have know your WHY.

My WHY was the literal survival of our church's ministry, my parent's legacy and my personal calling. The church had to change in order to adapt to the cultural forces of our new reality. This meant rethinking my leadership and the programs, ministries, and services of the church. It was truly an "innovate or die" situation. Now we are at a point where we are stronger, wiser, and even more motivated than before. Our leadership is more engaged and fully active in our growth process. New leaders have even joined with us as we continue our path of growth! All of this couldn't be done without knowing my WHY! In fact, all of this cannot continue without being willing to rethink my WHY? Your WHY changes as you change.

Today my WHY has changed from surviving to thriving! My purpose now is to maximize every gift God has given me to secure my family's future, increase the influence and impact of the Genesis Church globally, and help current and future generations of leaders in developing their potential and fulfilling their life's purpose worldwide.

Commit For the Long Haul

Another faith building essential is developing your capacity to commit for the long haul. King Solomon tells us in Ecclesiastes 3:1 there is *"a season, and a time, for every purpose under heaven."* He further states, there is *"a time to plant and a time to pluck up what's been planted (Ecclesiastes 3:2)."* Always remember, significant change requires significant time. Time to plant, take root, germinate and finally bloom. You must be prepared to encounter periods where you will see no tangible evidence of your plans working at all. I call these times - dry season. If you are not committed to the long haul, dry seasons will sap the life out of your vision and make you doubt your leadership. Committing to the long haul is essential to enduring such seasons and ultimately realizing your goals.

My Dry Season Encounter

I experienced a major dry season encounter during the construction of my church's family life center. It was the first time I endeavored into a building program. I was naïve about how much time and resources it would take in implementing this multi-million dollar project. I knew nothing about working with architects to develop plans, city planners for permits, and contractors to coordinate construction. This was on top of acquiring financing and running a capital campaign. In my haste I made the decision to have a ground breaking early on in the process thinking we would start construction in a few weeks or at the most a couple of months. I really made a big deal of it too sending out press releases, and inviting fellow Pastors, city officials, along with friends and family to the groundbreaking ceremony. It was a great occasion which was a capped off with the installation of a coming soon sign for the construction of the Dr. Robert Porter Center (DRPC).

First weeks passed, then months, then one year. By this time, the sign turned from a symbol of our promising future to a sad reminder of broken promises and major delays. We lost people and pledges as accolades turned into criticisms like "I told you it would never work" and "I knew those boys (my brother and I) didn't know what they're doing." Folks who we knew had our back walked away disappointed with the constant delays. But we kept the faith. We were committed for the long haul. My brother and I would flex our faith by preaching in detail about what the DRPC would look like and the great things we would be able to accomplish once completed. Finally after 2 years of going through several revisions of our plans, 4 banks for financing, and 3 contractors for construction we finally got the green light to start construction.

The first thing I requested was to tear down the "coming soon" sign!

Contagious Faith

Willingness to face adversity, knowing your WHY, and committing to the long haul leads to contagious faith! It is amazing how things turn around in your favor when you work your faith! The same people who oppose you will either start singing your praises - as if they have been doing so all along or simply vanish altogether. Those who stood with you will become your own personal evangelists, spreading the good news of your awesome leadership, incredible insight, and extraordinary vision. People will join your cause and contribute resources because they have caught what you have. YOUR FAITH has become contagious.

Credibility Equity

A direct benefit of contagious faith is the increase you receive in credibility equity. Everyone loves a winner, especially those who have won against the odds. Because of your victory and the proof of your faith people will give more value to your opinions, methods, and beliefs. You will achieve an undeniable mark of credibility in their eyes that was missing before. Understanding you now possess this increased equity of credibility is essential for leaders because you will need to leverage it in the future.

Leveraging Faith Credibility

After successfully constructing the Dr. Robert Porter Center we were able to immediately implement the various services and programs we originally planned. For seven years we were able to accomplish much of our personal and organizational goals. Our faith really paid off. However, I learned the full value of our faith credibility when another sign was placed on our property – a For Sale sign. Immediately people were worried, and some even frightened. We lost a few folk and people speculated about our future, but this time it was different. Our faith provided us credibility we could leverage during this adversity – and we did.

We went on the offense and let people know our faith was still strong and just like we believed God in past challenges, we believed God in this one. For a little over a year we were able to continue operating our ministry effectively in the community in our property- even with a For Sale sign on it. It wasn't easy, but our faith made it possible! After a year, the bank decided to take the For Sale sign down and negotiate with us plans for repurchase. Since that time we have been steadily on a path of growth and recovery. None of this could have happened without leveraging the credibility equity we received from working our faith in past challenges.

Be Strong & Courageous

> *"Be strong and courageous, because YOU WILL lead these people to inherit the land...."*
>
> *– Joshua 1:6*

Being a Unicorn in a Balloon Factory is a very challenging position and is not for the faint of heart. It will require significant sacrifice and risk in the face of incredible adversity. You will experience fear! Fear of the unknown; fear of not always having the answers; fear of the lack of resources; and fear of not being in control. Experiencing fear is not a sign of weakness. It is just being human. True strength and courage is not found in the absence of fear, but in the midst of it.

Bishop T.D. Jakes says, *"Courage is the will to do what you know to do in spite of the fear of doing."* [159] The key to being strong and courageous is facing your fear. The only way to get to your goal is by going through the very thing challenging your faith. My prayer for you is to not be overcome by the spirit of fear, but for you to rely on the power, knowledge and strength of God which resides in you! God only brings you tests you are meant to pass. You are in it to win it!

It won't be easy... but it is possible by FAITH!

References

AARP. "AARP: Leading a Multigenerational Workforce." *AARP.* 2010. http://assets.aarp.org/www.aarp.org_/articles/money/employers/leading_multigenerational_workforce.pdf.

Allison, Marion McClintic. *Organizational Structure.* 2001. http://www.enotes.com/business-finance-encyclopedia/organizational-structure (accessed 2010 12-September).

Ashkenas, Ron, Dave Ulrich, Todd Jick, and Steve Kerr. *The Boundaryless Organization: Breaking the Chains of Organizational Structure.* San Francisco, CA: Jossey-Bass, 2002.

Austin-Roberson, Kathleen. "Making Better, Stronger Churches Through Organizational Design." *Journal of Strategic Leadership* (Regent UNiversity) 2, no. 1 (2009): 27-39.

Bryan, Lowell, and Claudia Joyce. *Better strategy through organizational design.* May 2007. https://www.mckinseyquarterly.com/Better_strategy_through_organizational_design_1991 (accessed Feb 26, 2013).

Cassidy, J. "Me media: how hanging out on the internet became big business." *The New Yorker* 82, no. 13 (2006): 50

Center for Public Leadership. *National Leadership Index 2009: A National Study of Confidnce In Leadership.* Study, Harvard Kennedy School, Cambridge: Harvard Kennedy School, 2009.

Collins English Dictionary - Complete & Unabridged 10th Edition. "Dictionary.com." *Faith.* http://dictionary.reference.com/browse/faith (accessed March 5, 2013).

Collinson, Vivienne. "Leading by learning: new directions in the twenty-first century." *Journal of Educational Administration* 46, no. 4 (2008): 443-460.

Cornish, Edward. *Futuring: The Exploration of the Future.* Bethesda, MD: World Future Society, 2004.

Daft, Richard L. *Organization Theory and Design.* 10th Edition. Mason, OH: Cengage Learning, 2008.

Dalton, Dan, William Todor, Michael Spendolini, Gordon Fielding, and Lyman Porter. "Organization Structure and Performance: A Critical Review." *Academy of Management Review* 5, no. 1 (1980): 49-64.

Dwyer, Rocky J. "Prepare for the impact of the multi-generational workforce!" *Transformin Government: People, process and Policy* (Emerald Group Publishing Limited) 3, no. 2 (2009): 101-110.

Encyclopedia Britannica, Inc. "Faith." *Dictionary.com.* 2012. http://www.britannica.com/EBchecked/topic/200515/faith (accessed March 5, 2013).

Galbraith, Jay R. *Designing Organizations: An executive guide to strategy structure and process.* San Francisco, CA: Jossey-Bass, 2002.

Godin, Seth. *Tribes.* New york: Portfolio, 2008.

Griffin, Dana. "Tall Vs. Flat Organizational Structure." *Houston Chronicle.* http://smallbusiness.chron.com/tall-vs-flat-organizational-structure-283.html (accessed Oct 2012).

Handy, Charles. *The Age of Unreason.* Boston, MA: Harvard Business School Press, 1990.

Indrupati, Joel, and Tara Henari. "Entrepreneurial success, using online social networking: evaluation." *Education, Business and Society: Contemporary Middle Eastern Issues* 5, no. 1 (2012): 47-62.

Jakes, Thomas Dexter. "The Courage to Change Course." *Pisgah Experience.* Dallas: TD Jakes Enterprise, 2013.

Joiner, Bill, and Stephen Josephs. "Developing Agile Leaders." *INDUSTRIAL AND COMMERCIAL TRAINING,* 2007: 35-42.

Kotter, John P. *Leading Change.* Boston, MA: Harvard Business School Press, 1996.

Kouzes, J. M., and B. Z. Posner. *The Leadership Challenge.* 4th Edition. San Francisco, CA: Jossey-Bass, 2007.

London, Scott. "The Face of Tomorrow: Reflections on Diversity in America." *HopeDance Magazine* (Green Haven Press), Sept/Oct 1998.

McIntosh, Gary L, and R Daniel Reeves. *Thriving Churches in the Twenty-First Century: 10 Life Giving Systems for Vibrant Ministry.* Grtand Rapids, MI: Kregel Publications, 2006.

Miller, Calvin. *The Empowered Leader: 10 Keys to Servant Leadership.* Nashville, TN: B&H Academic, 1997.

Monroe, Myles. *In Charge - Finding The Leader Within.* New York: FaithWords, 2008.

Morgan, Gareth. *Imaginization: New mindsets for seeing, organizaing and managing.* San Francisco, CA: Berrett-Koehler Publishers, Inc., 1997.

Nadler, David A, and Michael L Tushman. *Competing By Design.* New York: Oxford University Press. Inc, 1997.

National Bureau of Economic Research. "Business Cycle Dating Committee, National Bureau of Economic Research." *National Bureau of Economic Research.* September 20, 2010. http://www. nber.org/cycles/sept2010.html (accessed July 12, 2012).

Northouse, P. G. *Leadership theory and practice.* 4th Ed. Thousand Oaks, CA: Sage Publication, Inc., 2007.

O'Toole, James. *Leading Change.* New York: Ballantine Books, 1995.

Qualman, Erik. *Socialnomics: How Social Media Transforms The Way We Live And Do Business.* Hoboken, New Jersey: John Wiley & Sons, Inc., 2009.

Raines, Claire. "Managing Millennials." *I Can Still Do That.* 2002. http://icanstilldothat.org/about/reverse-mentoring/managing-millennials-by-claire-raines/ (accessed July 19, 2012).

Raines, Claire, and Arleen Arnsparger. *Millenials at Work.* 2010. http://www.generationsatwork.com/articles_millennials_at_work.php (accessed July12 2012).

Rodriguez, Richard. "The Browning of America." *PBS.* Feb 18, 1998. http://www.pbs.org/newshour/essays/february98/rodriguez_2-18.html (accessed July 19, 2012).

Rosenthal, S A. "National Leadership Index 2011: A National Study of Confidence in Leadership. ." *Harvard Kennedy School Center for Public Leadership.* December 2011. http://www.hks.harvard.edu/leadership (accessed August 2012).

Selman, Jim. "Leadership and Innovation: Relating to Circumstances and Change." *The Innovation Journal.* 12 12, 2002. http://www.innovation.cc/discussion-papers/selman.pdf (accessed 9 4, 2012).

Simons, Tony L. "Behavioral integrity as a critical ingredient for transformational leadership." *Journal of Organizational Change Management* 12, no. 2 (1999): 89-104.

Thomas, Greg. *Leading "Generation X" Workers.* 2004 September. http://www.leadingtoday.org/Onmag/sepoct04/genx92004. html (accessed 2009 16-November).

Toor, Shamas-ur-Rehman, and Stephen Ogunlana. "Ineffective leadership: Investigating the negative attributes of leaders and organizational neutralizers." *Engineering, Construction and Architectural Management* 16, no. 3 (2009): 254-272.

United States Census 2010. http://2010.census.gov/2010census/ (accessed 2011 11-14-April).

Wikipedia contributors. *In Living Color.* The Free Encyclopedia. Wikipedia. July 13, 2012. http://en.wikipedia.org/w/index. php?title=In_Living_Color&oldid=502130599 (accessed July 13, 2012).

—.*It's the economy, stupid.* July 10, 2012. http://en.wikipedia.org/w/index. php?title=It%27s_the_economy,_stupid&oldid=501577057 (accessed July 19, 2012).

—. *Tiger Woods.* July 6, 2012. http://en.wikipedia.org/w/index. php?title=Tiger_Woods&oldid=500998332 (accessed July 13, 2012).

Winston, Bruce. *Be a leader for God's sake.* Virginia Beach, VA: Regent University, 2002.

About the Author

Dr. Tecoy Porter Sr. is the lead Senior Pastor of the Genesis Church in Sacramento, CA, were he has served faithfully since 1999. He holds a Doctorate of Strategic Leadership degree from Regent University's School of Business and Leadership, and a Master's of Business Administration degree from California State University, Sacramento. Dr. Porter is also an adjunct Professor at William Jessup University's School of Professional Studies in Rocklin, CA and Epic Bible College Graduate School where he instructs in their business and leadership programs. An emerging voice in the field of Christian leadership, Dr. Porter often serves as an expert author, workshop instructor, panelist, and keynote speaker in the areas of leadership development, economic empowerment, gospel music, and the state of the church.

Dr. Porter has authored three books: *Releasing Your Inner Treasure: 8 Kingdom Keys to Unlocking the Wealth Within You (2007); Treasure Chest Collection Vol.1: Inspirational Reflections for Abundant Living (2009); and his latest release, Faith To Innovate: 21st Century Tools & Strategies for Leadership Transformation.* An accomplished choir director, producer and songwriter, Dr. Porter, along with his brother Dr. Ellington Porter, has released 5 musical recordings featuring the award winning Genesis Church Music Ministry under their independent label Markee~Wes Productions.

Dr. Porter is an ordained member of Bishop T.D. Jakes' Potter's House International Pastoral Alliance (PHIPA) and serves as lead over the

Ecclesiastical Council of the Edwin & Walter Hawkins Music & Arts Love Fellowship Pastors. With the launch of the Mukono Prayer Palace in Kampala, Uganda in 2010, Dr. Porter extended his ministry internationally conducting crusades and clinics affecting thousands.

Prior to his pastorate, Dr. Porter was employed in the Information Technology field as a trainer, manager, and consultant to a variety of companies in Northern California. In March of 2001, he retired from his career in Information Technology to work fulltime in the ministry.

Dr. Tecoy Porter is blessed to share his life with his lovely wife, Karlette Porter and his 3 children: sons Tecoy Jr., Kamarion, and daughter, Kara. You can learn more about Dr. Porter at *www.drtecoyporter.com* and *www.sacgenesis.org*.

(Endnotes)

1   Rosenthal, S A. "National Leadership Index 2011: A National Study of Confidence in Leadership." Harvard Kennedy School, Harvard University, Cambridge, 2011, 1-16.

2   Rosenthal 2011, 4.

3   Monroe, Myles. *In Charge - Finding The Leader Within.* New York: FaithWords, 2008.

4   Kotter, John P. *Leading Change.* Boston, MA: Harvard Business School Press, 1996.

5   Joiner, Bill, and Stephen Josephs. "Developing Agile Leaders." *Industrial And Commercial Training*, 2007: 35-42.

6   Toor, Shamas-ur-Rehman, and Stephen Ogunlana. "Ineffective leadership: Investigating the negative attributes of leaders and organizational neutralizers." *Engineering, Construction and Architectural Management* 16, no. 3 (2009): 254-272.

7   Joiner and Josephs 2007, 35.

8   Northouse, Peter Guy. *Leadership: Theory and Practice.* Thousand Oaks: SAGE Publications, 2007, 3.

9   Simons, Tony L. "Behavioral integrity as a critical ingredient for transformational leadership." *Journal of Organizational Change Management* 12, no. 2 (1999): 89-104.

10   Center for Public Leadership. *National Leadership Index 2009: A National Study of Confidnce In Leadership.* Study, Harvard Kennedy School, Cambridge: Harvard Kennedy School, 2009.

11   Daft, Richard L. *Organization Theory and Design.* 10th Edition. Mason, OH: Cengage Learning, 2008, 389.

12   Northouse 2007, 346.

13   Northouse 2007, 358.

14   Kouzes, J. M., and B. Z. Posner. *The Leadership Challenge.* 4th Edition. San Francisco, CA: Jossey-Bass, 2007.

15   Kouzes and Posner 2007, 34.

16   *Ibid*, 35-36.

17   *Ibid*, 36.

18   Selman, Jim. "Leadership and Innovation: Relating to Circumstances and Change." *The Innovation Journal.* 12 12, 2002. http://www.innovation.cc/discussion-papers/selman.pdf (accessed 9 4, 2012).

19   Collinson, Vivienne. "Leading by learning: new directions in the twenty-first century." *Journal of Educational Administration* 46, no. 4 (2008): 443-460.

20   Cohen, Stephen L. "Effective global leadership requires a global mindset." *Industrial and Commercial Training* 42, no. 1 (2010): 3-10.

21   Cornish, Edward. *Futuring: The Exploration of the Future.* Bethesda, MD: World Future Society, 2004, 204.

22   Cornish 2004, 213.

23   Winston, Bruce. *Be A Leader For God's Sake.* Virginia Beach, VA: Regent University, 2002, 5.

24   Miller, Calvin. *The Empowered Leader: 10 Keys to Servant Leadership.* Nashville, TN: B&H Academic, 1997, 8.

25   Wikipedia contributors. *It's the economy, stupid.* July 10, 2012. http://en.wikipedia.org/w/index.php?title=It%27s_the_economy,_stupid&oldid=501577057 (accessed July 19, 2012).

26   National Bureau of Economic Research. "Business Cycle Dating Committee, National Bureau of Economic Research." *National Bureau of Economic Research.* September 20, 2010. http://www.nber.org/cycles/sept2010.html (accessed July 12, 2012).

27   Ibid

28   Wikipedia contributors. *In Living Color.* The Free Encyclopedia. Wikipedia. July 13, 2012. http://en.wikipedia.org/w/index.php?title=In_Living_Color&oldid=502130599 (accessed July 13, 2012).

29   Rodriguez, Richard. "The Browning of America." *PBS.* Feb 18, 1998. http://www.pbs.org/newshour/essays/february98/rodriguez_2-18.html (accessed July 19, 2012).

30   U.S. Census Bureau. *United States Census 2010.* 2010. http://www.census.gov/prod/cen2010/briefs/c2010br-02.pdf (accessed 2011 13-July).

31   U.S. Census Bureau 2010.

32   Wikipedia contributors. *Tiger Woods.* July 6, 2012. http://en.wikipedia.org/w/index.php?title=Tiger_Woods&oldid=500998332 (accessed July 13, 2012).

33   London, Scott. "The Face of Tomorrow: Reflections on Diversity in America." HopeDance Magazine (Green Haven Press), Sept/Oct 1998.

34   Raines, Claire, and Arleen Arnsparger. *Millenials at Work.* 2010. http://www.generationsatwork.com/articles_millennials_at_work.php (accessed July12 2012).

35   Raines, Claire. "Managing Millennials." *I Can Still Do That.* 2002. http://icanstilldothat.org/about/reverse-mentoring/managing-millennials-by-claire-raines/ (accessed July 19, 2012).

36   Raines and Arnsparger, Millenials at Work 2010.

37   AARP. "AARP: Leading a Multigenerational Workforce." AARP. 2010. http://assets.aarp.org/www.aarp.org_/articles/money/employers/leading_multigenerational_workforce.pdf.

38   AARP 2010.

39   Thomas, Greg. *Leading "Generation X" Workers.* 2004 September. http://www.leadingtoday.org/Onmag/sepoct04/genx92004.html (accessed 2009 16-November).

40   Dwyer, Rocky J. "Prepare for the impact of the multi-generational workforce!" *Transformin Government: People, process and Policy* (Emerald Group Publishing Limited) 3, no. 2 (2009): 101-110.

41   *Ibid*, 105.

42   Qualman, Erik. Socialnomics: How Social Media Transforms The Way We Live And Do Business. Hoboken, New Jersey: John Wiley & Sons, Inc., 2009.

43   Cassidy, J. "Me media: how hanging out on the internet became big business." *The New Yorker* 82, no. 13 (2006): 50.

44   Indrupati, Joel, and Tara Henari. "Entrepreneurial success, using online social networking: evaluation." *Education, Business and Society: Contemporary Middle Eastern Issues* 5, no. 1 (2012): 47-62.

45   socialbakers.com

46   Qualman 2009, 2.

47   *Ibid*, 3.

48   Indrupati and Henari 2012.

49   Qualman 2009, 14.

50   Blume, K. Allen. "'Guilty as charged,' Dan Cathy says of Chick-fil-A's stand on faith." *The Biblical Recorder*, July 2, 2012.

51   Foust, Michael. "Chick-fil-A interview with BR triggers media storm." *Baptist Press*, July 19, 2012.

52   Lyons, Gabe. *The Next Christians: The Good News About the End of Christian America*. New York: Random House, 2010.

53   Lyons 2010, 20.

54   *Ibid*, 23.

55   The Barna Group. *Americans Are Creating the New American Dream*. June 28, 2011. http://www.barna.org/culture-articles/500-americans-are-creating-the-new-american-dream (accessed July 3, 2011).

56   Olsen, David T. *The American Church In Crisis*. Grand Rapids, MI: Zondervan, 2008.

57   Pew Research Center's Forum on Religion & Public Life . *"Nones" on the Rise: One-in-Five Adults Have No Religious Affiliation* . Survey, Washington, D.C.: Pew Research Center, 2012.

58   Pew Research Center's Forum on Religion & Public Life 2012

59   Barna Group 2011.

60   Olsen 2008, 58.

61   The Condition of the Church in America - Key Statistics www.p2pministry.com/p2phome_files/church_condition_2.htm

62   Lyons 2010, 26.

63   Stoltzfus, Tony. Leadership Coaching - The Disciplines, Skills and Heart of a Christian Coach. Virginia Beach, VA: Tony Stoltzfus, 2005, vii.

64   Kimsey-House, Henry, Karen Kimsey-House, and Phillip Sandahl. *Co-Active Coaching: Changing Business, Transforming Lives.* 3rd. Edited by Kindle. Nicholas Brealey Publishing, 2011.

65   Kimsey-House, Kimsey-House and Sandahl 2011, 3.

66   International Coaching Federation. *Overview & FAQ.* 2011. http://www.coachfederation.org/about-icf/overview/ (accessed September 3, 2011).

67   Stoltzfus 2005, 7.

68   Harkavy, Daniel. *Becoming A Coaching Leader.* Nashville, TN: Thomas Nelson Publishers, 2007.

69   Fournies, Ferdinand F. *Coaching for improved work performance.* New York: McGraw-Hill, 2000, 12.

70   *Ibid*, 12.

71   Zenger and Stinnett 2010.

72   International Coaching Federation 2011.

73   Ibid

74   Zenger and Stinnett 2010.

75   ICF, 2011.

76   Stoltzfus 2005, 46.

77   *Ibid*, 21.

78   *Ibid*, 53.

79   Zenger and Stinnett 2010.

80 Crane, Thomas G. The Heart of Coaching: Using Transformational Coaching to Create a High Performance Coaching Culture. San Diego, CA: FTA Press, 2010, 12.

81 Stoltzfus 2005, 68.

82 Longenecker, Clinton O. "Coaching for better results: key practices of high performance leaders." *Industrial and Commercial Training* 42, no. 1 (2010): 32-40.

83 Wright, Susan, and Carol MacKinnon. *Leadership Alchemy: The Magic of the Leader Coach.* Toronto: TCP Publications, 2003, 5.

84 Raines, Claire. "Managing Millennials." *I Can Still Do That.* 2002. http://icanstilldothat.org/about/reverse-mentoring/managing-millennials-by-claire-raines/ (accessed July 19, 2012).

85 Harkavy, Daniel. *Becoming A Coaching Leader.* Nashville, TN: Thomas Nelson Publishers, 2007, 158.

86 Kimsey-House, Henry, Karen Kimsey-House, and Phillip Sandahl. *Co-Active Coaching: Changing Business, Transforming Lives.* 3rd. Edited by Kindle. Nicholas Brealey Publishing, 2011, 33.

87 *Ibid*, 33.

88 Manktelow, James, and Amy Carlson. *Active Listening.* http://www.mindtools.com/CommSkll/ActiveListening.htm (accessed 1 2013).

89 Kimsey-House, Kimsey-House and Sandahl 2011, 35.

90 *Ibid*, 36.

91 Stoltzfus, Tony. Coaching Questions- A Coach's Guide to Powerful Asking Skills. Virginia beach, VA: Tony Stoltzfus, 2008, 6.

92 Harkavy 2007, 158.

93   Harkavy 2007, 60.

94   Stoltzfus, Tony. *Leadership Coaching - The Disciplines, Skills and Heart of a Christian Coach*. Virginia Beach, VA: Tony Stoltzfus, 2005, 81.

95   *Ibid*, 82.

96   Whitmore, John. Coaching for Performance-Growing People, Performance, and Purpose. London: Nicholas Brealey Publishing, 2002.

97   National Football Foundation. *Hall of Fame Inductee - Eddie Robinson*. 1997. http://www.footballfoundation.org/Programs/CollegeFootballHallofFame (accessed February 4, 2013).

98   Stoltzfus 2005, 80.

99   Rogers, Carl. *On Becoming A Person*. Boston: Houghton Mifflin, 1961.

100 Daft, Richard L. *Organization Theory and Design*. 10th Edition. Mason, OH: Cengage Learning, 2008, 58.

101 Dalton, Dan, William Todor, Michael Spendolini, Gordon Fielding, and Lyman Porter. "Organization Structure and Performance: A Critical Review." *Academy of Management Review* 5, no. 1 (1980): 49-64.

102 McIntosh, Gary L, and R Daniel Reeves. *Thriving Churches in the Twenty-First Century: 10 Life Giving Systems for Vibrant Ministry*. Grtand Rapids, MI: Kregel Publications, 2006, 174.

103 Nadler, David A, and Michael L Tushman. *Competing By Design*. New York: Oxford University Press. Inc, 1997.

104 Daft 2008,

105 McIntosh and Reeves 2006, 173

106 Austin-Roberson, Kathleen. "Making Better, Stronger Churches Through Organizational Design." *Journal of Strategic Leadership* (Regent University) 2, no. 1 (2009): 27-39.

107 Daft 2008, 93.

108 Ibid

109 Griffin, Dana. "Tall Vs. Flat Organizational Structure." *Houston Chronicle*. http://smallbusiness.chron.com/tall-vs-flat-organizational-structure-283.html (accessed Oct 2012).

110 (Ashkenas, et al. 2002)

111 Allison, Marion McClintic. *Organizational Structure*. 2001. http://www.enotes.com/business-finance-encyclopedia/organizational-structure (accessed 2010,12-September).

112 Griffin n.d.

113 Ibid

114 Morgan, Gareth. *Imaginization: New mindsets for seeing, organizaing and managing*. San Francisco, CA: Berrett-Koehler Publishers, Inc., 1997.

115 Galbraith, Jay R. Designing Organizations: An executive guide to strategy structure and process. San Francisco, CA: Jossey-Bass, 2002, 37.

116 Bryan, Lowell, and Claudia Joyce. *Better strategy through organizational design*. May 2007. https://www.mckinseyquarterly.com/Better_strategy_through_organizational_design_1991 (accessed Feb 26, 2013).

117 Bryan and Joyce 2007

118 Ibid

119 Ibid

120 Ibid

121 Ashkenas, Ron, Dave Ulrich, Todd Jick, and Steve Kerr. The Boundaryless Organization: Breaking the Chains of Organizational Structure. San Francisco, CA: Jossey-Bass, 2002.

122 Daft 2008, 120

123 Handy 1990, 40

124 Daft 2008, 125

125 *Ibid*, 127

126 Nadler and Tushman 1997, 8

127 Katzenbach, Jon R, Ilona Steffen, and Caroline Kronley. "Cultural Change That Sticks." *Harvard Business Review*, Jul - Aug 2012: 2-9.

128 Daft, Richard L. *Organization Theory and Design*. 10th Edition. Mason, OH: Cengage Learning, 2008, 374-375.

129 Cameron, K S, and R E Quinn. *Diagnosing and Changing Organizational Culture*. San Francisco, CA: Jossey-Bass, 2006, 16.

130 Daft 2008, 375.

131 Cameron and Quinn 2006, 17.

132 Banks, Roert, and R Paul Stevens. *The Complete Book of Everyday Christianity*. Downers Grove, IL: InterVarsity Press, 1997.

133 Daft 2008, 376.

134 Northouse, P. G. *Leadership theory and practice*. 4th Ed. Thousand Oaks, CA: Sage Publication, Inc., 2007, 177-178.

135 Banks and Stevens, 1997.

136 Wren, J Thomas. The Leader's Companion: Insights on Leadership Through the Ages. New York, NY: The Free Press, 1995, 281.

137 Ibid

138 Shein, Edgar H. *Organizational Culture and Leadership: A Dynamic View*. San Francisco: Jossey-Bass,1991, 23.

139 Cameron and Quinn 2006, 117.

140 *Ibid*, 144.

141 Kent, Robert H. *Installing Change.* 2ndEdition. Winnipeg: Pragma Press, Inc., 2001.

142 Katzenbach , Steffen and Kronley 2012, 3.

143 Kotter, John P. *Leading Change.* Boston, MA: Harvard Business School Press, 1996, 36.

144 Moran, John H, and Baird K Brightman. "Leading organizational change." *Career Development International* 6, no. 2 (2001): 111-118.

145 Daft 2008, 436.

146 *Ibid*, 437.

147 Kotter 1996, 145.

148 Kent 2001.

149 Kotter 1996, 137.

150 Rogers, Everett M. *Diffusion Of Innovation.* New York: Free Press, 2003, 281.

151 Kotter 1996, 148.

152 *Ibid*, 156.

153 Connerley, Mary L, and Paul Pedersen. Leadership in a deverse multicultural environment: developing awareness knowledge and skills. Thousand Oaks, CA: Sage Publications, 2005, 2.

154 Godin, Seth. *Tribes.* New York: Portfolio, 2008, 72-73.

155 Northouse, P. G. *Leadership theory and practice.* 4th Ed. Thousand Oaks, CA: Sage Publication, Inc., 2007.

156 Collins English Dictionary - Complete & Unabridged 10th Edition. "Dictionary.com." *Faith.* http://dictionary.reference.com/browse/faith (accessed March 5, 2013).

157 Encyclopedia Britannica, Inc. "Faith." *Dictionary.com.* 2012. http://www.britannica.com/EBchecked/topic/200515/faith (accessed March 5, 2013).

158 Qualman, Erik. *Socialnomics: How Social Media Transforms The Way We Live And Do Business.* Hoboken, New Jersey: John Wiley & Sons, Inc., 2009.

159 Jakes, Thomas Dexter. "The Courage to Change Course." *Pisgah Experience.* Dallas: TD Jakes Enterprise, 2013.